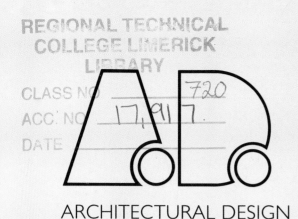

ARCHITECTURAL DESIGN

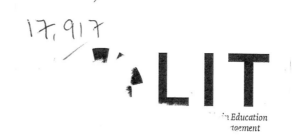

LIT
Education
...gement

EDITORIAL OFFICES:
42 LEINSTER GARDENS, LONDON W2 3AN
TEL: 071-402 2141 FAX: 071-723 9540

EDITOR
Dr Andreas C Papadakis

EDITORIAL TEAM: Maggie Toy (House Editor), Vivian Constantinopoulos, Nicola Hodges, Helen Castle
DESIGN TEAM: Andrea Bettella (Senior Designer), Mario Bettella, Sharon Anthony, Owen Thomas
SUBSCRIPTIONS MANAGER: Mira Joka, BUSINESS MANAGER: Sheila de Vallée

CONSULTANTS: Catherine Cooke, Terry Farrell, Kenneth Frampton, Charles Jencks, Heinrich Klotz, Leon Krier, Robert Maxwell, Demetri Porphyrios, Kenneth Powell, Colin Rowe, Derek Walker

SUBSCRIPTION OFFICES:
UK: VCH PUBLISHERS (UK) LTD
8 WELLINGTON COURT, WELLINGTON STREET
CAMBRIDGE CB1 1HZ UK

USA: VCH PUBLISHERS INC
SUITE 909, 220 EAST 23RD STREET
NEW YORK, NY 10010 USA

ALL OTHER COUNTRIES: VCH VERLAGS-GESELLSCHAFT MBH
BOSCHSTRASSE 12, POSTFACH 101161
6940 WEINHEIM GERMANY

CONTENTS

Lucinda Lambton

Nicholas Ward-Jackson and Anish Kapoor

Exchange House, Broadgate

Bengal House in the City of London

Quinlan Terry, Bengal House in the City of London

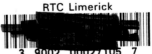

THE LUCINDA LAMBTON DIARY

Flats in Waltham Green, East London and Schweitzer's House, California

Forlornly scouring the British Isles for perfect modern housing, I am forever on the look-out for clever, colourful, crisp and clear-cut lines whose originality will quite slice into the senses. The lesson that sheer and stark forms, however modest, need never be mean, is one that we should learn forthwith, before yet another ingredient is added to the pastiche pudding.

  I am not throwing it out of the kitchen – the richer the better as far as I am concerned – but having once given myself the supreme treat of eating nothing but puddings washed down with cream and custard for three days, I have learnt the value of a balanced diet. I fear, too, that it is much easier to enjoy the comforting old recipes than it is to create something entirely new. The feast of vernacular that is covering the land is soothingly safe and should be relished to the full but we must spice it up with buildings that are unquestionably of our own time. Good modern buildings of modest means could and should become part of our daily fare. It is modest rather than monied modernity that seems to be the key issue for change and I know of only two examples that I can hold up as exemplary, one in Waltham Green, the other in California. The first is Julian Wickham's small development of flats on the edge of Waltham Forest in East London and the second is Josh Schweitzer's house in the high desert of the Joshua Tree National Monument, east of Los Angeles, both of them built in 1990. Both have strongly sculptural forms, are simple and small, yet vibrantly singing of today, curiously enough in the same vivid tones. The brilliant blue and terracotta have in fact been bitter bones of contention with the neighbours of 20b Bisterne Avenue, London E14. When the tenants moved in Julian Wickham had an open day when, according to Kitty Birch who lives on the ground floor, there was a babble of 'very offensive comments', with one woman in particular shouting 'Get rid of the paint, get rid of the paint!' And this cauldron of controversy is still ludicrously boiling today. When I photographed the building, I was jeered by the mildest looking man as to whether I was: 'Filming a horror story?'. The local vicar had valiantly weighed into the fray, writing to the chief planner that the colours were exciting and alive and that the flats should be an inspiration to other local authorities. And so they should, with their sleekly substantial detailing: the waving wall, the porthole windows and the Crow's Nest which looks out over the forest. Most important of all, every one of the flats is built so that the sun rises into the bedrooms and sets on all six of the sitting rooms. The proof of the pudding is surely in the eating and Kitty enjoys a good gorge every day; 'That awful woman at the open day. I'd have bopped her, if I'd been Julian. All I can say is that if you get up here in the morning and you've got the hump, you only have to look outside and it cheers you up!'

In California, Josh Schweitzer's house quite pierces you through with its precise yet unsterile simplicity. Its primitive forms and colours, at the same time both architectural and indigenous, seem to sprout strangely out of the very land on which they are built. With the green of the cactus and the yucca, the orange of the desert flowers and the purple-blue of the distant ridges, all the vivid hues of the seemingly monochrome desert are built into these stark little blocks in their great stark landscape. Each tiny building is a different room; the orange walls are only a shelter, in which you are wrapped round by the warm air, as you gaze out over the great desert vistas through the astonishing and as-yet-only-to-be-seen-in-children's-drawings doors and windows. The green sitting room gives the same fractured views of the rocks and the sky, as does the bedroom, all in their wonderfully warped way. Being there is like magically wandering into a futuristic paradise, at once simple and dream-like.

Hugh Colvin's Buildings

You do not generally expect to be tuned into thigh tingling delight by the morning post. All letters offer an adventure as different worlds open up with each envelope, but seldom do their contents whirl you into instant inspiration and delight. Such was the effect of Hugh Colvin's letter, with illustrations to match the marvellous news that he was making ceramic architectural models in every conceivable and most covetable form. From three inches high to two feet high, with the Connolly Folly at Castletown in Ireland and the great pyramidal mausoleum by Bonomi at Blickling in Norfolk; he has made over five hundred brilliant little buildings, listed and priced as if they were everyday merchandise! What a spree it would be to order the Desert de Retz Pillar House or the Casino at Marino in Dublin by Chambers, as well as the Triangular Lodge by Sir Thomas Tresham or an arch by Inigo Jones.

Imagine being be able to concentrate the passion for architecture into the palm of the hand and what a pleasure it would be to gather all these models together and to consummate that passion by recreating one of those great amalgams of architecture that were painted in the 19th century. They are pictures that have every style crammed onto their canvasses and here was a chance to do the same with a photographic print. *The Architect's Dream* by Thomas Cole in Toledo Ohio, would be a perfect example to follow, with its pyramids and porticos, its towers and its spires all rising up to the sky ; as would *The Professor's Dream* by CA Cockerell at the Royal Academy with its 74 buildings and monuments on their 'Medieval, Roman, Greek and Egyptian Levels'; otherwise any of Sir John Soane's schemes that were painted by Joseph Gandy, all of them architectural dreamscapes, jam-packed with the different orders. A great adventure lay ahead – I arranged for Hugh Colvin to bring as many of his buildings as he could muster up and together we would scale the higher echelons of architectural art! He appeared, with a Shangri-la of buildings in the back of his van and together we created our dream townscape. Although many of his models are miniatures of existing buildings, others are not and have been made with only the help of the architects' unrealised drawings and plans. It is an enchanting thought, for example, that Gibbs' temples from his *Book of Architecture* has now at long last been built in three-dimensional form. Some extant buildings, altered over the years, have been 'rebuilt' by Colvin, such as the Boycott Pavilion at Stowe, which was given a octagonal dome by Borra in the middle of the 18th century. Others have been demolished and re-created from drawings or old photographs, with the counting of bricks as the only clue for scale.

Hugh Colvin himself is the architect of other more fantastical buildings, such as the stylised collapsing Italianate pile called The Earthquake Hotel, richly redolent of the Best chain of supermarkets throughout America. His is the great success story, with the new Heinz Architectural Centre of the Carnegie Museum at Pittsburgh planning to buy everything that he has ever made in the past and everything that he will ever make in the future. They have also suggested that he produce all 52 of Wren's towers and spires! This, incidentally, is the lively proposition of one Patrick Horsbrugh, an English architect living in the United States, who was responsible for moving Wren's St Mary's Aldermanbury to America and for rebuilding it stone by stone at Westminster College in Fulton, Missouri, in 1964, on the site of Churchill's Iron Curtain speech. Anyway, back to Hugh Colvin, who must be praised to the skies. He is, as

far as I know, the only man to have ever produced ceramic architectural models of such exquisite and unerring perfection on such a scale. There have been classical ruins in cork, marble and soapstone, there have been ceramic and shell cottages and churches galore and there have, of course, been a multitude of 'one offs' such as Wrens masterpiece model of St Paul's and Lutyens' of Liverpool Cathedral. Even as you read these lines today, the finishing touches are being put to a giant model of Winchester Cathedral made out of matchsticks. Never, however, has such precision been perfected, if not for a mass then at least for a modest market. The Emperor of Japan is a lucky man and The Queen Mother a lucky woman, who have both been presented with these architectural gems. So too am I, now the proud possessor of Bonomi's pyramid spiking up in sharpest splendour, with both it and I having bid a mournful farewell to all the other beauties as they were borne back with Hugh Colvin to his workshop in Wales. I craved and still do crave for each and every one of them to be crammed into my own house – a permanent 'Architect's Dream' through which to waft daily. Anyone could realise it for themselves by ringing 0547 520339, or by writing to The Old School House, Llanfairwaterdine, Knighton, Powys. Colvin's father is Howard Colvin, the king of architectural historians and author of the newly published and much acclaimed *Architecture and the After-Life*. With such scholarship encouraging him from the wings as it were, Hugh Colvin's life was always set fair for a remarkable architectural performance.

A La Ronde, Devon

Hurray for a sympathetic audience, when each nuance of your talk is rewarded with such tangible responses that they leap back onto the stage like encouraging slaps on the back. One feeds the other and on you charge, audience and speaker with an ever growing momentum of mutual satisfaction. Such was my happy lot in the vast and hideous Great Hall of Exeter University, when giving a talk on curious houses and most particularly on A la Ronde, the little 16-sided 'Cottage Ornée' built by two spinster cousins, the Misses Jane and Mary Parminter in the 1790s. With a stroke of brilliant bravery, as it is quite unlike any other house in their care, the National Trust have recently acquired this strange little building and the talk was to help raise money for its restoration.

A la Ronde is one of the most extraordinary houses in all England; indeed I would go so far as to say that it is one of the most extraordinary houses in all the world. Modelled on the 16th-century Byzantine basilica of San Vitale in Ravenna but riddled through with secular rather than ecclesiastical gaiety, it was built by the two ladies as a culmination of their ten-year long Grand Tour of Europe. It is like a giant Cabinet of Curiosities; outside with diamond shaped windows cut with the sharp contours of the walls and inside with as strange a mix of architecture and artifacts as you are ever likely to see.

There are triangular rooms narrowing down to three inches at their apex, friezes of game birds' feathers, a shell grotto that bulges out of the fireplace and an hexagonal hall, round which all the rooms revolve. Hidden away in all eight of the hall's elegantly marbled door-cases are secret benches to be swung down for extra comfort when sitting out a dance. But it is upstairs where A la Ronde reveals her greatest secret of all. You open a strangely narrow door into a tiny grotto of a gothic staircase, with all the magical strangeness that one might dream of only as a child. With its shoulder-width walls and its shallow steps that slope forwards, you are forced to bend forwards as up you squeeze, past fossils, shells and mirrors embedded into the walls. Up you scrunch, between walls ablaze with glistening protruberances, past a house of quills and a curious shrine. On and up you go, into A la Ronde's crowning glory: a shell, bone, feather, sand and china encrusted gallery. It is an explosion of rarity; razor shells zig-zag, feathers are laid as birds and limpets as petals of flowers. There are minerals, fossils and wax seals, one fir cone, a teapot spout and even a horse's neck bone; each and every one laid out with meticulous care, in patterns as well as tableaux and pictures, with some thousands of shells decoratively pronouncing the architectural lines. It took 'the ladies' 11 years to create this icon to individuality and when they had finished they painted a great crown over the entrance to the gallery, both to celebrate the Golden Jubilee of George III and Queen Charlotte the following year and of course to proclaim their great triumph of having built A la Ronde. The Misses Parminter were a hundred years before their time, like two great Victorian pioneers, single-handedly blazing away with their little house. The National Trust should be congratulated for saving such a singular building and we should do all that we can to ensure that every pheasant's tail and every limpet shell is restored to its former glory. Even the 18th-century chocolate bought by the ladies, and part of their brimful cabinet of curiosities, should remain intact for eternity.

STUART LIPTON

INTERVIEWED BY

MAXWELL HUTCHINSON

My philosophy is quite simple – we're all in this. You decide who are the players and you have relationships – all different kinds – and they are over time.

A wretched row of new terraced houses, just south of the River Thames, mark a turning point in contemporary British architectural patronage.

A patch of barren land caught between the Old Vic, the homeless cardboard hell of Waterloo Bridge, Denys Lasdun's National Theatre and the Festival Hall shaped the priorities and established the critical dogma of a still young Stuart Lipton, arguably Europe's single most influential architectural patron.

Coin Street goes down in early 1980s architectural mythology. It was a little known Lipton's road to Damascus. He admits that his Coin Street scheme was the turning point in his understanding and development of a rounded attitude to architecture and his choice and patronage of architects.

The land had been lying vacant for longer than most can remember. Certainly since the war. A useful place to park the car on a visit to the National Film Theatre or the Hayward Gallery. Marginalised. Not by its absolute urban geography – no further from Trafalgar Square than Centrepoint, but by the insoluble intervention of the River Thames.

Lipton, who had been in property, one way or another, all his life, was then running the property company Greycoat jointly with Geoffrey Wilson. He was little known although he had already been noticed in the cafe society of a newly flourishing London architectural scene.

Cutler Gardens in the City of London and 250 Euston Road had already shown his developing interest in architecture and, more importantly, his individual power to pay and engage the architects.

The long established commercial firm of Scott Brownrigg and Turner beat a path to Lipton's door with an idea to unlock part of the blighted land by the river at Waterloo. Lipton immediately recognised the potential of the location. But his vision went further than that and certainly beyond the simplistic solutions of

Lansdowne House, Berkeley Square

architectural commercialism. As the land was owned by the Greater London Council, very much in the public domain and under the control of the London Borough of Lambeth as planning authority, Lipton recognised, through his experiences at Tolmer's Square, north of the Euston Road in Camden, the need for public consultation. The need not only for real estate solutions but for architecture which would win hearts and minds, and the all important Planning Consent.

The Coin Street Community was already mobilised under the leadership of Ian Tuckett. The battle lines were drawn long before Lipton saw beyond the Scott Brownrigg & Turner ideas.

Since starting the property company Sterling Land with the same Geoffrey Wilson in 1971 Lipton had enjoyed the company of architects. He set himself publicly aside from his competitors through a conspicuous and developing interest in the art of architecture and the arts in general. Some said that this showed commercial weakness. To be counted amongst the architectural cognoscente would surely not go down well with the City?

Coin Street gave Lipton the opportunity he needed to test his developing ideals about architectural quality twinned with a new transparency in the development process, engaging all comers with a disarming frankness.

Lipton had known Richard Rogers for some time. He respected and admired Rogers' work at the Beaubourg in Paris. Particularly the way in which an uncompromising contemporary building addressed its surroundings and created public spaces which were new, fresh and inviting.

Lipton initially engaged Scott Brownrigg & Turner. But it quickly became clear that there was only a chance to win planning approval with a comprehensive design for all of the 12-acre site. He changed the brief to a comprehensive development and saw the need for a different architectural approach. Rogers was his man. In that single gesture he took the all important step from commercial architectural expediency to philanthropic architectural idealism.

Lipton seems quick and ready to learn. Even today after 25 years in the property and development business. On the Coin Street drawings at Richard Rogers' then small office in Holland Park he found the perfect tutor with the manner, patience, pace and realism to articulate the architectural process with just the right degree of persuasion and commitment.

Rogers produced the now legendary scheme. A liquid progression of galleries snaking their way from Waterloo Station to the banks of the Thames and, admittedly idealistically, over a new bridge to the North Bank and the City beyond. Shades of things to come with his National Gallery extension scheme and the urban design plan to link Trafalgar Square to the South Bank via the new bridge which featured so stunningly in the Royal Academy Exhibition.

It was Rogers' idea to produce a mixed development, 20 percent housing, 80 percent split between offices and commercial use. The locals wanted housing and gardens for the entire site. Rogers proposed mixed uses which would create a structural magnet on the south side of the river which, combined with the South Bank Arts Complex, would create a new lively centre and in so doing regenerate a larger area of South London.

The drawings, as ever, were stunning, if a little difficult for the untrained eye. Just as the original design drawings for the Pompidou Centre owed much of their graphic heritage to the Pop treatment (Ron Herron and Peter Cook) of the Archigram group. Hardly the ready medium for consultation in the lull before the storm of public opposition.

Lipton was shrewd enough to recognise that his architect alone could not carry the scheme through public criticism. He too had to stand four square behind the ideas and in so doing needed the confident language of expression and counter criticism.

The Coin Street scheme was launched with great skill. Architect and client stood shoulder to shoulder in the perfect conviction of their ideas. Skilfull, contemporary, uncompromising architecture which, according to an increasingly self-confident Lipton worked commercially, despite the apparent complexity of its construction and novelty of its ideas. Lesser developers would have weakened at the thought of new construction techniques and clashing uses and left the land alone or, worse still, set their architect up as Humpty-Dumpty to go it all alone.

The buildings themselves were only part of the Rogers/Lipton Coin Street concept. The public spaces around and about the buildings were its community contribution. Lipton recognised this as one of the scheme's greatest potential achievements.

At every Coin Street meeting, from the hair-raising battle ground of local public meetings, through the reverential solemnity of the RIBA lecture theatre to the endlessly protracted legalities of the Public Enquiries, Rogers and Lipton were inseparable. And so emerged a new paradigm for contemporary architectural patronage.

Michael Heseltine, on his first tour of duty as Secretary of State for the Environment granted two Planning Consents, one to Greycoat the developers, the other to the local action group. Greycoat decided to drop the scheme, for commercial reasons, when Lipton left in 1983.

The houses that stand there today bear echoing witness to the missed opportunity and the nonsense of building artisan cottages within a stone's throw of St Paul's.

Lipton did not need to lick his wounds. There were none.

All great architecture the world has known owes its genesis, in one way or another, to self-conscious patronage. From the Pharaohs' pyramid of Cheops to Mitterrand's courageous pyramid in the Place Napoleon.

In that span of almost three thousand years architecture has relied upon the courage and commitment of a range of commissioning patrons. From the unselfish individual, through the totalitarian materialism of the state to the image-making aspirations of commerce and business.

The state, the church – religion in general – and powerful dynasties account for the vast proportion of historical patronage. Certainly, the vast majority of European architecture can be divided in this way. Take any great European city, separate out its churches and religious buildings, the buildings of state and municipality and the private palaces and indulgences of the aristocracy, and little other than architectural flotsam remains.

At least until the 20th century. The Victorians added little to the mechanism of architectural patronage – but pointed the way forward to the new potential of commercial patronage. The emergent railway companies satisfied their sense of self importance with station buildings. Commerce, industry and enterprise built utilitarian but dignified mills and factories and the more enlightened philanthropic industrialists like Lever and Cadbury started a process of individual patronage which led us forward to the late 20th century.

As a contemporary patron, Lipton is an enigma. As a property developer he breaks the mould of fast talking, quick dealing, shallow greed and ambition.

He has an uncompromising physical presence. Large and seemingly ungainly he is shockingly quiet spoken, thoughtful and attentive – despite his reputation for firmness and rumours of short temper and impatience.

The self-effacing Lipton cannot even call to mind the year in which he was made an Honorary Fellow of the Royal Institute of British Architects – a rare honour for a property developer and certainly for one who is still one year short of his 50th birthday.

25 years of successful development, the leadership of no less than three publicly quoted property companies and a list of development schemes second to none in the recent history of the British property industry, makes him one of the wealthiest men in property. The *Sunday Times* 'Book of the Rich' rates Lipton as worth £89 million and adds, 'He sold his company, Sterling Land for £28 million a month before the property crash in 1973. "I was simply lucky," he says of that time'. His 10 percent share in Sterling Land helped pave the way for patronage despite the 75 percent fall in Stanhope shares in the property recession of the late 1980s.

Opulent but tasteful offices in the Saatchi and Saatchi headquarters building by Chapman Taylor on the west side of Berkeley Square are no less than would be expected for a large publicly quoted property company and certainly more spacious and elegant than the majority, thanks to Eric Parry's understated design.

As a contemporary patron, Lipton is an enigma. As a property developer he breaks the mould of fast talking, quick dealing, shallow greed and ambition . . .

Lipton learnt the need for stage management and communication – even for propaganda

Lipton himself still lives in the same house in St John's Wood he bought in 1973. No country house, no yacht, no racehorses but a growing and distinguished personal art collection.

Our patron seems to satisfy the creative urge of patronage through a catalogue of obvious achievement. And maybe also from membership of the Royal Fine Art Commission, and positions on the Board of such institutions as the National Theatre. This is no Donald Trump or John Portman – just a developer with a stunningly perceptive eye for just the right architecture. At least in the main.

Lipton started training as a Chartered Surveyor and, in his own words, 'chickened out'.

By his own admission he had no interest in architecture until the 1970s. Everything, in the beginning, was about creating the right space for the customer, the tenant. Real estate for real estate's sake. All stacking up neatly with a 'healthy bottom line'.

He carried out his own first development in 1970, discovering his own natural proclivity for detail. He turned out a small scheme distinguishing itself from its competition. He chose the doorknobs, the light fittings, the carpets and the sanitary fittings. And still does today.

In 1971 at the age of 29 Lipton set up Sterling Land with Geoffrey Wilson. Wilson seemed to know a lot more about architecture and knew more architects. As ever, Lipton was a fast learner. From then on Lipton became increasingly conscious of the need to use the best architects he could find – or at least the best architects about which he knew or whom he had met.

In his long early portfolio he singles out the Collett's building at 127-133 Charing Cross Road by Michael Lyall. He whispers unfamiliar language about shadows, form and context. Then in 1972 Taylor of Chapman Taylor built the tall black tower at the end of Pentonville Road, King's Cross. Chapman took just a moment away from the developer-led architecture to introduce Lipton to the idea of buildings and sculpture with a nice piece of work by Bill Pye.

In 1972 at Henrietta Street in Covent Garden, Sterling Land came face to face with well orchestrated public opposition. Lipton set up exhibitions and public consultation meetings. The public comments book was stolen. The meetings were angry. Lipton learnt the need for stage management and communication – even for propaganda. He lost the day and the Courts of Covent Garden were never built.

In 1973 Wilson and Lipton sold Sterling Land and in 1976 set up Greycoat. Michael Lyall designed the Hammersmith International Centre for which Lipton suddenly uses a new language of description. This, for him, is unequivocally 'a distinguished building'.

The battle ground of Henrietta Street led naturally to the fight for Tolmer's Square on the Euston Road across Hampstead Road from the Euston Tower. Nick Waites made a formidable adversary fighting hard for social housing and eventually winning some, if not all, of his aspirations. Waites was generous enough to comment about Lipton: if you have to have a developer, this is the developer to have.

Gerald Levine of Renton Howard Wood Levine produced an uncompromisingly contemporary mirror-glass building, now occupied by the Prudential Insurance Company. Lipton had by now learnt enough to understand the building and to stick by his architect despite the obvious complexity of its construction and its conspicuous lack of conformity with the office forms of its time.

And then, in 1979, came Cutler Gardens in the City of London. Richard Seifert, who at that time had built more buildings in London than anyone since Sir Christopher Wren, brought the scheme to Lipton: 800,000 square feet of office space. Lipton eulogises about the public spaces with landscaping by Russell Page which clearly sowed the seeds for the public domain at Broadgate, Stockley Park and maybe even (if we are lucky) at King's Cross.

Strengthened by the success of Tolmer's Square and Cutlers Gardens, (and a myriad of smaller and less well known schemes) Lipton, in 1979 at the age of 37, was ready to come out of the closet as an individual patron and take on the challenge of Coin Street. The bedrock of Lipton's self confident architectural patronage is founded on nine enduring principals. He would not recognise these himself but they are recurring leitmotifs of Wagnerian proportion. If he did understand them as explicitly, or could articulate them, much of his native craft would be diminished.

His early life as an estate agent in the City taught him 'that the customer knows best'. Regardless of the quality of a building, if it does not satisfy the tenants' needs it will stay on the pages of the *Estates Gazette* week after week. So Lipton puts the user first. And he damn well makes sure that all his architects understand that.

The experiences at Henrietta Street, Tolmer's Square and Coin Street have taught the lessons of public consultation. Good clear drawings, beautiful models, propaganda leaflets and brochures, all help win public support and understanding of sophisticated architecture, of increasing complexity and modernity.

That buildings cannot exist *in vacuo* seems evident after the flush of urban design studies as far reaching as those for the Isle of Dogs, Stockley Park, Terry Farrell's frozen ideas for the rejuvenation of London's South Bank, and the idealism of the King's Cross twilight zones. Lipton has learnt that a broader view, beyond the site and the building, pays dividends. Setting a building in a broader context, understanding the ripple effect of redevelopment helps reinforce the identity and significance of the individual within the group.

Eric Parry Building, Stockley Park

Fourth in the unwritten Lipton code comes construction technology. In 1983, following 1 Finsbury Avenue (to which I will return), he left Greycoat, parting with Geoffrey Wilson with whom he had worked for nearly 14 years and took a sabbatical year. Much of which was spent in America studying construction, in particular the up-to-date use of the steel frame and dry construction. Quick as ever to learn, he imported this technology, and in the case of many of the early Stanhope buildings some of the engineers whom he had met, particularly in the field of mechanical services and air conditioning.

Today's Stanhope boasts that it can build buildings with everything other than the architectural ideas – the all important creative stimulus which Lipton recognises must be left to the architect. The company employs quantity surveyors, engineers, building surveyors – an entire team who scrutinise every nut, bolt, beam, pipe and duct of Lipton's carefully wrought schemes.

This in-built understanding of construction technology leads inexorably to the company's approach to quality control. Lipton talks about 'no happier moment than sitting down with the architect, working at the drawings'.

Then there is financing, which I guess Lipton would not claim as his sole prerogative. Geoffrey Wilson and the others clearly did their bit in arranging the money at Sterling Land. In the Lipton/Wilson partnership at Greycoat we can but guess that Wilson played a major role in arranging money, just as he has done more recently with Terry Farrell's Charing Cross building and the development money for Neo-Classical Paternoster Square. By Lipton's own admission, Godfrey Bradman, one side of Rosehaugh of the binary partnership with Stanhope, was responsible for raising the £1,200 million it has taken to build Broadgate. And a lot more besides.

The Lipton that emerged from the skirmishes of Coin Street is a man that recognises architectural merit on its own terms seemingly regardless of style. The man that can commission, in the same breath, Norman Foster, John Outram, Terry Farrell, Ian Ritchie and Troughton McAslan, has a catholic architectural taste. One by which he is prepared to stand or fall commercially.

Next comes his self confessed and enduring position as a Modernist. He would surely like to build his own house one day? And who would be the architect? 'I am unashamedly a modernist'. And again: 'My wife is probably one step behind me in modernism'.

And finally, in the Lipton catalogue of mine we include heroism. Not just the courage to put his architectural money where his mouth is, often to withstand public criticism, in the case of King's Cross and the Arups scheme for Paternoster Square, but also to speak out against his critics including the Prince of Wales.

Stanhope were chosen as the Project Managers for the original Paternoster Square redevelopment. They held a competition. Arups Associates won. An exhibition was held in the crypt of St Paul's. Arups' concept drawings used all Lipton skills in public communication, but in this instance, by his own

Exchange House, Broadgate

admission, took some risks with the public's potential understanding of complex architectural ideas in a particularly sensitive and reverential setting. He tabled just the initial masterplan without the details of building styles. The public were clearly not ready to participate at such an early stage. Their simple level of criticism needed clear images of fully designed buildings.

The exhibition was hijacked by the London Evening Standard newspaper, who commissioned John Simpson to produce a neo-classical scheme. Simpson's model was cleverly infiltrated into Lipton's exhibition in the crypt of St Paul's and courtesy of the propaganda clout of a daily newspaper, swung public attention away from the sensibly and equitably arranged competition in favour of the pretender.

Lipton is coy about this episode in recent Stanhope history. No uncalculated words of criticism of His Royal Highness, rather a steadfast modernist reaffirmation in the principals of originality and novelty: 'I find it difficult to comprehend how anyone can really bring back traditions which no longer exist. If I asked you if you wanted an original or a reproduction most people would go for an original.' Despite his public position in the Royal debate (which he welcomes) he regrets that the development industry and the architectural profession have not managed to find someone with an equally accessible voice to respond to the debate with authority and balance.

Surely a pious hope in a country increasingly riddled with the ossifying mortality of monarchy.

That catalogue from user needs through quality control, urban design, construction technology, modernity and personal heroism adds up to today's Stuart Lipton formula. It is not a formula frozen in time. It has developed from a simple conversion in Mayfair to the anticipation of the King's Cross millennium vision.

The 1983 sabbatical in the States came at just the right time. Refreshed and invigorated by the transatlantic experience – particularly procurement methods and technology – Lipton returned from the United Kingdom and set up Stanhope Securities.

1 Finsbury Avenue, was just finishing. This first hint of the masterplanning exercise for the redevelopment of Liverpool Street Station at Broadgate was his last contribution to the Greycoat portfolio. He had appointed Arups Associates, Sir Philip Dowson and Peter Foggo, to tackle one of the most valuable sites in one of the most expensive Cities in the world.

Award winning 1 Finsbury Avenue speaks for itself. A delicate and gracious building which established a new language for large floor plan buildings in the wake of big bang and the reorganisation of the financial management of the City of London.

Lipton talks lucidly about 'the external realm and the private realm, the form, the function, the light and the shadow'. Little does he realise the resonance with classic architectural teaching about which he clearly knows very little. He has learnt it from all those architects whom he has engaged over the years.

Following the success of 1 Finsbury, British Rail approached Lipton, amongst others, for ideas on the redevelopment of Broadgate over the railway lines of Liverpool Street. They suggested that he team up with Godfrey Bradman whose Rosehaugh company had already made a reputation for imaginitve financial and funding arrangements.

Rosehaugh/Stanhope took on the challenge with alacrity. Lipton engaged Arups. Peter Foggo headed up a team fresh from the success of 1 Finsbury.

Surprise, surprise, they ended up in the last two taking on the might of Norwich Union head on. They won, as we can see. In 1984 Rosehaugh/Stanhope took on the first four phases of Broadgate building: a total of 1.7 million square feet in a remarkable 12 months per phase using the American construction techniques Lipton had learnt during his year out.

The Arup buildings develop the architectural concepts and language of 1 Finsbury. The elevations of the uncompromisingly large Broadgate buildings are fractured, broken and articulated in a startlingly innovative way. Typical of the Lipton approach the Broadgate Arena, with its winter ice-skating rink and public spaces, set the buildings in an intelligent context and give over much of the precious land to public use.

The early phases of Broadgate were completed just before the British property industry reached melt-down. At the height of construction the Arups phases at Broadgate were reputedly the fastest spending construction site in Europe.

Where Lipton and Bradman turned their minds to the latter phases of the scheme, along the Bishopsgate frontage, Arups had reputedly spent their energy and were already turning their minds to Stockley Park and other Lipton schemes.

On his trips to America Lipton had visited Chicago, met Bruce Graham of SOM and had been impressed by their experience of building over railway tracks, tackling very large buildings quickly and marshalling vast technical resources particularly those associated with dry American construction and computer-aided design.

Broadgate Arena

SOM were appointed for the remaining phases of Broadgate. The buildings which came out of the London office of SOM, backed up by the resources from Chicago, are in stark contrast to the Lipton ideal of the early Arups phases. Gone are the delicate approaches to mass form, shape, cladding and elevation.

SOM were understandably new to the London property and planning scene. They were encouraged by the City Planning Officers to use stone and to follow the railway vernacular. Lipton admits that: 'One has moments when you think of the task as well as thinking of the architecture'. An uncharacteristic lapse of judgement and taste.

Each of the Bishopsgate buildings in the SOM scheme is round about 600,000 square feet of gross office space. Three buildings totalling 1.8 million square feet. Plus the Exchange building with its dramatic arch spanning over railway lines below which adds up to a further 400,000 square feet.

Lipton admits the architectural shortcomings of this part of his portfolio describing them, *sotto voce,* as 'Late Empire'.

To be generous, he can be forgiven this oversight, given the enormous pressures of producing Broadgate, at such a magnitude, and such financial risk, in such a short period of time. Moreso as Broadgate was only a tiny part of the post Coin Street Stanhope revelation.

Despite competition and spurious claims from the unlikely geography of Tampa or even Seoul, London's Heathrow airport remains the busiest in the world.

A mile or so away from Terminal One and the ever-congested tunnel under the runways, a rubbish tip in the London Borough of Hillingdon has been transformed into one of the most architecturally significant Business Parks in the world.

The idea of turning acres and acres of putrefied urban detritus into business parkland was Peter Jones' of Trust Securities. Lipton bought a share in the company, engaged Arups Associates, yet again, to produce a masterplan. All that in the blistering heat of Broadgate at full pace.

Stockley Park has only just started. In 1985, under the watchful eye of an Arup masterplan already including buildings by Norman Foster, Ian Ritchie, SOM, Eric Parry, Geoffrey Dark, Troughton McAslan, with Richard Rogers, Arup Associates and Peter Foggo waiting on the drawings for the latter phases.

The Lipton nine-point plan has its most consummate manifestation at Stockley with no compromise. Each building is a gem and the concept masterful and unerring.

The layout, the landscaping, the circulation and the uncharacteristic unity of the buildings by different architects within Arups' intelligent and subtle masterplan makes Stockley a world class development. A pace-setter for things to come.

One of the things to come is the new Lipton scheme for a business park at Chiswick with a master plan by Terry Farrell, The Lipton/Farrell relationship is a new one. Farrell has yet to build anything for him. Their first partnership conjured up the re-development of London's South Bank Arts Complex with a not always praised or welcomed scheme including considerable demolition, funded by commercial development which many saw in conflict with the primary artistic intent.

Ian Ritchie Building, Stockley Park

Farrell's Chiswick scheme has just kicked off the starting blocks. It will include buildings by many on the now well tried and trusted Lipton list plus Farrell and ABK. Many have credited Lipton for encouraging Farrell to move on from the obvious post-modernism of Charing Cross and Alban Gate to a fresher neo-modernism.

And meanwhile Broadgate, and meanwhile Stockley Park, the Lipton/Bradman partnership dreamt up and continue to support the King's Cross redevelopment on the back of the new Channel tunnel terminal in the heart of London. With fierce competition against, amongst others, Trevor Osbourne and Speyhawk, the Norman Foster masterplan with its new urban parkland, social housing, and soaring office towers confronts the narrow minded opposition of the Local Authority. Lipton believes it will still happen despite recent decisions about the re-routing of the Channel tunnel railway line.

PS As if that lot were not enough take a look on the Grays Inn Road, at Norman Foster's building for ITN, another Lipton scheme which shows the mature Sir Norman with his most consummate and skilful command of late 20th century British modernism.

And despite this aerobic output Lipton continues to remain, at least on the surface, calmly in command of all that he surveys.

There are rumours about divorce, or is it marriage, between Lipton's Stanhope and Bradman's Rosehaugh. Both companies are making losses in the decimated property industry of the early 1990s.

Whilst Bradman looks concerned, based as he is in the financial end of the property market, Lipton, with mother architecture at his side, continues to sound quietly confident.

For sure, he is surrounded by many architect friends who will continue to support his idealism if, for no other reason, that they owe him a living and the opportunity to develop British architecture beyond their wildest dreams.

He puts much of his success down to a particular personal relationship with the architects with whom he works. He knows them socially. They visit his office regularly. He takes a deep interest in their work, to the extent that he has recently published his own company magazine, 'Foundation', featuring their work and encouraging architectural journalism and criticism albeit for sound commercial propaganda reasons.

But strangely and worryingly he is taciturn about his architectural knowledge and the foundation of his architectural understanding and commitment. He seems to know little about contemporary architectural history, struggles to find heroic buildings of the Modern Movement with which he can identify. When asked what really counts in making good architecture, he trots out a three point plan more typical of a Chartered Surveyor than a single individual who has so successfully encouraged some of the best British buildings since the war. He puts it simply: 'The needs of architecture are very simple and they haven't changed for three centuries: a clear brief, a specification and a good set of drawings'. How can he say that, and only that, when he can put his name to this architectural catalogue?

It is difficult to get to the heart of the man. Yes, he likes music but finds it difficult to say what he likes. His language is comfortingly clear of the usual dialectic of architectural discussion. He is known, increasingly, as a collector of Fine Art, the London School, including works by Auerbach, Leon Kossoff, Kitaj, Raymond Mason. Asked for the aesthetic underpinning for his taste his reasons come back quite simply: 'the pictures give him pleasure'.

Well, maybe for today's patron and connoisseur that quiet self confident inarticulate preference is just fine. Just enough, some would say refreshingly free of rhetorical post-rationalisation.

Heaven forbid that Stuart Lipton's secretary should ever lose grip on his diary. Or for that matter, that the man himself should have a whimsical desire to throw an extravagant dinner party for all his architects. Together at one time regardless of their proclivities.

For a start, Sir Richard Rogers and Terry Farrell would be forced to bury the hatchet on their dispute over the future planning of London. After all, Lipton was footing the bill for dinner and their fees.

John Outram and Ian Richie could swap their own approach to New Ageism as mystically divided as they are by neo-Egyptian and spiritual structuralism. Sir Norman Foster would find it a little difficult to swap philosophical posturing with Bruce Graham with only the English language to help. Meanwhile the rest of the bunch, Troughton McAslan, Peter Foggo, Geoffrey Dark, and most of the rest of British architecture's contemporary *Who's Who*, would have a ball discussing yet another commission from the Magus at the head of the table who would probably have little to say but know that he still had a lot to learn. And who could do a lot worse than pop back to Coin Street and reprise the experience which turned a simple surveyor into this country's architectural impressario *par excellence*.

... a single individual who has so successfully encouraged some of the best British buildings since the war

ITN Building, Gray's Inn Road

XVII

THE BERLIN CITY FORUM

Architectural Design Magazine had a rare opportunity to video record the entire proceedings of the extraordinary Berlin Stadtforum Symposium held in August 1991. The Stadtforum provides a regular opportunity for people to discuss planning strategy for Berlin and this forum brought together architects, philosophers, economists, historians, film-makers and other interested parties as well as the citizens of Berlin.

Here we present extracts of the discussion of the forum between Kurt W FORSTER, Director of the Getty Centre for the History of Art and Humanities who also writes and lectures extensively on Modern architecture in Europe and the USA, Akira ASADA, an economic theorist who works on concepts and ideas that emerge from economics and embeds economics in the largest possible picture of human activity, and Jacques DERRIDA, the French philosopher who has expanded his study of language in the most comprehensive fashion to the study of historic life. He teaches in Paris and at the University of California, Irvine.

The complete proceedings will be published in the near future, for further information please call Clare Telfer at Academy Group on 071-402-2141.

FORSTER: We are trying in this symposium to bring together people coming from different parts of the world with a wealth of experience, with a rich tradition of critical thinking and imagination so that our guests are really forced to focus on those problems which are emerging. I think most of us have some kind of link with Berlin, are familiar with Berlin and its problems, but to set some highlights and in order to sort of penetrate into the city at some given point and familiarise ourselves specifically with aspects which might tend to get lost in the overall picture during the past hours of the morning we have gone on a tour of this city showing various points of interest here which might lead to quite a few questions.

However it might be useful to sum up in a few words the definition of this institution. Within such a forum, the most encouraging thing may be the mutual collective engagement, and thereby the creation of a public forum, in which everybody can freely participate to the hilt – to the extent of their knowledge, of their intelligence, and their capacity to take hold of the problems in discussion. At the same time, there is probably a somewhat frustrating dimension to this, in that this parliament usually disbands at the end of the deliberations but it does not enter by itself in the the next chapter and actually execute the results of its proceedings. This is an enormously disciplined procedure whereby a maximum participation is required, but a rather restricted and qualified result will come out of the proceedings themselves.

I believe frustration is natural to this forum and its limitations are symbolic of the frustrations that everybody experiences in urban life, namely that they are always on a building site. The transformations are not only disruptors and measures of the incompleteness, they are also an absolutely necessary state. In fact, they are the guarantee of the life of the city. In that sense, this city is now experiencing such an on-rush of life that normal procedures in tools and defenses seem to be inadequate or frustrating, or perhaps even disappointing.

I'd like to ask the members of this symposium to give us a brief assessment of things that struck you the most, that come to the fore, that impose themselves on your mind as you go through the city, as you acquaint yourself, as you have, with the life and presence of this town. May I ask Akira to try to break the ice?

ASADA: Well, first of all I have to say that I feel quite at a loss what to do now because I'm an alien here in many senses of the word. First of all, I am Japanese. This is only my third visit to Berlin, the first one after the wall fell, and, at the same time, I'm an alien because I am not specialised in urban planning, architecture, etcetera. Therefore, I feel a little awkward to speak about the city of Berlin in front of specialists like you.

FORSTER: In the United States they make television series about aliens because only aliens can explain what's going on around them.

ASADA: Yes, if a city is anything, it is a place where aliens can come and exchange ideas and thoughts with each other. A city is basically a place of exchange and people tend to think of the city as a kind of closed community, but it's false because the city is primarily a place of exchange and 'exchange', as Marx put it in *Das Capital*, 'begins where the communities end.' The exchange begining between communities and the city, as a place of exchange, is a kind of enlargement of this inter-space – this space in-between communities. This is especially true to Berlin, the city between East and West, the city where the people from all over the world can meet and exchange ideas with each other.

Therefore, this forum, including me and Jacques Derrida as aliens, can be a kind of micro-model of the city itself, and it is only in that sense that I can hope to contribute to thinking about the city in a somewhat new dimension. Now, going back to the impression of Berlin as I saw it under the wonderful guidance of Kurt Forster, I was especially struck by the polycentric and multi-layered structure of the city. It is not a city governed by one single centre or two or three centres, it is a particularly polycentric city. Kurt Forster talked about islands or enclaves, each with its proper characteristics. These enclaves or islands, are not

Jacques Derrida and Kurt W Forster

only isolated from one another, there are inter-spaces between them and we can see a kind of multi-layered overlapping of many dimensions and many characteristics. Therefore, I was very much struck by this polycentric, multi-layered structure of the city and the basic question it seems to me, is how to develop this structure in a more polyphonic, creative way.

FORSTER: May I ask Jacques Derrida to engage in the same theme?

DERRIDA: I could say the same thing Akira Asada said about being an alien and not only an alien, but I feel very incompetent in terms of architecture, urbanism, and so on and so forth. But as a preliminary remark I would say, first, how grateful I am for having been invited to such an exemplary experience as *Stadtforum*. I think it's perhaps, to my knowledge, the first time that such a conference takes place. As if a city – an old city with an enormous history and enormous memory – acts as if it was in the process of re-founding itself, re-building itself anew. And as you, everybody knows, when an event of foundation takes place, of course, there is no law, there are no premises; in fact the foundation as such inaugurates something, doesn't simply develop or continue the past. It has no time to give anyone. That's what the active foundation implies. But at the same time, of course this is not true, Berlin has not to be refounded – it is already founded. So this is the first paradox of this *Stadtforum* which acts as if we were at the eve of a new city which has nevertheless to take into account an enormous

heritage. The fact that you invite – I am talking of you the German citizens – aliens and somehow incompetent aliens to participate in this reflection, means a lot in general, and to me. Today, founding a building or re-founding something like a city implies a responsibility which has itself to be redefined. What is a responsibility? In what way are we responsible? In front of a city or for a city, in front of whom are we responsible? Who is responsible for what? I would claim that especially in the case of Berlin, the responsibility has to be shared by a number of an indeterminate people – by an indeterminate number of people, politicians, experts, citizens of Germany, but also perhaps by non-citizens. To put it briefly, what is the name of Berlin – what is the identity of Berlin. Of course I was struck by the polycentric, the multiplicity, the multi-layered structure of Berlin, nevertheless this multiplicity has a limit of course. You cannot simply continue to multiply the multiplicity. There is something enigmatic called Berlin that has reference and at least a possible identity, a past identity which was enigmatic because it was already divided, already polycentric, and so on and so forth. We feel we are responsible for Berlin. Now, not only in the way we are today responsible for a number of capitals of rich historical capitals as in Paris, Vienna, Prague, Moscow, but because of what happened in Berlin in recent times. For what are we responsible? That is the question I am asking myself and in general. This morning during the tour I was struck also by the discontinuity, the heterogeneity and by the dilemma of what to do with

these scars on the skin of the city. To conceal something in memory would be significant not only for Germany but for the Western world first and for the world in general as a whole. So, I am going to jump directly to what is to me, as an incompetent philosopher, the problem of decision-making in such a situation. You insisted a moment ago, on the time pressure and, when a decision has to be made, there is, structurally, a problem of time pressure. There is no decision without time pressure, however long the time is. The decision is always precipitated by the concrete problems dealt with by the experts of space, housing transportation, etcetera and the so-called fundamental topics: philosophical and political. Generally speaking, of course there is a gap: and I would like to insist on this gap. (Of course, I am on the side of the non-expert). It goes without saying that, in such a situation, when you have to make responsible decisions you must of course be an expert – or at least you have to consult the experts. Non-scientific, non-expert decisions would be irresponsible; that's obvious. But at the same time, on the other hand, no expert as such can make a decision, and take historical, political and ethical responsibility. The decision cannot be made by an expert , but by someone who is not in the situation – not an expert. So as far as our responsibility towards the city of Berlin is concerned – the name of Berlin, of past Berlin or future Berlin, the supposed identity of the references; this responsibility has to be taken by an inner body, in the situation of *not* being an expert. So who are the non-experts in that case? Who

are the non-architects, the non-urbanists, the non-etcetera. The immediate answer is the citizens, German citizens, the citizens of Berlin, the constituency, the representatives of the city of Berlin, but not only them. Of course they have to be part of it and I think that the fact that this *Stadtforum* is open to the public, that it's transparent and it welcomes anyone is a good sign. But I think that for historical reasons, non-citizens of Berlin, non-citizens of Germany may have some-thing to say and to share in the decision-making, not simply in decision-making in the technically political term, but in the advice they can give to these decision-makers. I think the fact that we are here in a strange theatre with the dark here on one hand and light on the other, is symbolic. Between the light, the supposed light, enlightenment or knowledge of the experts and the non-knowledge of the situation in which decisions are made, there must be a gap. And this abyss is not reducible, it is structural, even if it's the expert as such who makes the decision: between his expertise and the decision-making there must be an irreducible and infinite gap and I think that discontinuity is very significant in the current situation of the *Stadtforum* of Berlin. I think that when the *Stadtforum* got under way, the decision of giving Berlin the status of the capital of Germany was not made. It has been made now and of course this decision will have enormous consequences on the topics we are dealing with here. There is no problem about that, but I would have liked Berlin to have been spared this fate as the city would have been freer to witness everything. Now, with political centrality the city will have all these witnessings will be more difficult.

FORSTER: You hit on a whole range of themes, many of which will certainly occupy us. I would like to take up one of the things that Jacques Derrida mentioned when talking about the re-foundation of the city. Cities have various stages in their existence – they assume critical new functions like the function of a capital city or the seat of particularly significant institution and therefore, in a sense, re-configure themselves in order to play that new role. There have been stages in history in various places where a gradual enlargement of similar functions have occurred, as opposed to others and other conditions when a re-foundation was felt to be necessary – the kind of hypothetical new start – and of course there could hardly be a condition imaginable which would have a more compelling reason for a hypothetical fresh start than the city of Berlin itself. Its entire historic condition cried out for this. So re-foundation – what does a re-foundation mean? What would be the acts by which the city is re-founded? What would be the decisions and the ideas that underlie such a re-foundation?

DERRIDA: I really do not know. And this non-knowledge implies something I would like to define. Of course, the only law of this re-foundation, if it is the re-foundation of an already existing city bearing the name of Berlin, is the law of Berlin. Berlin is the law. Something named Berlin is the law and we are before the law in that case. This means that being responsible

doesn't mean being responsible to something present. We are responsible for 'past' Berlin and the enormous memory of Berlin and you know how many layers, proper names, works, this memory entails. And we are responsible to all of them – all of those ghosts. We have to be true to them – but they are not present, they are ghosts – neither living nor simply dead. We have a responsibility to these ghosts and responsibility to the country, the future inhabitants of Berlin. But not only the inhabitants of Berlin, future subjects interested or concerned or sharing some concern for Berlin. So there is no other law. If there is a law it has to be called Berlin, if it has some singularity, some originality. Now, if I said I was regretting the decision of transferring the capital to Berlin, it is for many reasons, and I won't be able to discuss all of them. I think that today, what has been called the city age, is finished. We enter as someone said, in a past city age and of course, a capital today is not simply a solid structure in terms of walls, buildings, and so on; it is a certain mode of concentration of capitalism, of money, of means, of information, of decision-making. All this doesn't occur only in a geographical site, but everywhere. Some concentration occurs and our responsibility is to be vigilant, about any re-constitution of mono-centric capital. This doesn't mean that we can or should simply erase or destroy any capital or capitalistic fear, because it's through some concentration in terms of information, money, teaching, culture, that for instance, democracy can be kept alive. I think that the double bind (including the element of indecision), the

double obligation for Berlin would be to keep the memory, unity, some centrality and the tradition of the city but, – and this is of course a self-contradiction, but I think that self-contradictions have to be assured, accepted here – a decision which doesn't go through some indecision, undecidability, isn't a decision. A decision which simply follows a number of premises, is not a decision.

A decision has to go through some impossibility of coming to a decision, some double-bind. And the double-bind here is to keep of course, the memory, the unity, the tradition, some centrality and at the same time, build something which contradicts this centrality. We can juxtapose the traditional solid concrete buildings and memories and archives without transforming Berlin into a museum.

FORSTER: It may be very useful in a sense, to return to the question of the re-foundation because there is a very important historic precedent. I don't want to bore anybody, but there are innumerable instances that I could specifically identify and discuss as to what measures were taken, and what effect resulted from the deliberate incision in the body of an existing city. For instance, the transformations – almost all of them by now wiped out of course – in the centre of Berlin made between 1815 and 1840. This amounts to nothing less than a re-foundation and re-definition of the entire centre of Berlin. Not even in London could you have a corridor which would end with the *Bau Akademie* at the one end, and would lay out in a panoramic fashion, all the major institutions brought into relief by the planning of

Schinkel (and mind you, not accomplished by drawing a masterplan) and then taking 25 years to do it, but by only addressing each instance, individually as in our selected case, and only over time, as it were, building more than the sum total of what these individual things amount to. So this re-foundation could be very helpful for a discussion of what interventions are imaginable, not so much where would you put it or what would it be, but also the means; you mentioned iconography. The term iconography by the way historically emerges from maps and views, not from icons. So the interesting thing there is that you have the most astonishing reversals. Today it is probably the highest privilege to be the lowest building among high-rises. Perversely, because you're sitting on the biggest pot with the smallest ass. There are many instances where in fact today, in American cities the government buildings and the truly central institutions are recognisable for being low-rises surrounded by a forest of tall buildings. I just want to say that the fact that the highest is automatically to be identified with the most potent or the most conspicuous etc, may not hold in all circumstances.

DERRIDA: If we don't need tall buildings it's because of the fact that power is not, today, identified with stone and space but with information: technological information processes, telephone connections and so on. That's why the identity of the city, and of anything today, cannot be measured with solid stone, but with technical power and technical devices. So the map is not the essential part in the conception of a city and the location of a building is not the essential part of it. I also want to mention the paradoxes of foundation and re-foundation. First, foundation and re-foundation should not be something that's thought of as something romantic – exceptional let's say, happening once and for all. The foundation and the re-foundation of the cities happen every day. Why? First because as soon as a foundation is supposed to have taken place, it has to be repeated in the same tradition – the concept of foundation implies the concept of re-foundation. So, where the tradition is inscribed in the very concept of foundation, so a foundation is always a re-foundation or claims to refer to a previous foundation. This is at the same time very abstract and formal and very concrete because each time you do something to a city – say you change a street, you add a monument or you open an avenue – you transform the whole context and you, in some way, re-found it.

Now, that's why re-foundation is never self-foundation. I will claim that there is no self-foundation. To found oneself you have to be already founded, otherwise, you wouldn't found yourself. To found yourself, you have to be other than yourself and that's why the function is always in the hands of some other; be it the state, the future, from anywhere. But there is no set foundation and self-foundation is always of course, an ideological claim. So the general question is – what does belonging mean – belonging to a city. What is in the city – what is located in the city, what is visible, what is not visible, and sometimes what is not visible may belong to the city, but it is not necessarily located in the

physical sense in the city. To whom does that telephone wire belong? The very concept of belonging to what we call a city is a problem and of course, everything we discuss here presupposes, that we should know what can be identified with the building, with the name 'building', with the limits of the city. What are the limits of the city? Of course we know today what the administrative limits are and what the inner limits are – the different limits of the sections, the neighbourhood, for there are some visible limits. But who can seriously define the absolute limits of a city?

ASADA: I noticed that this city looks to me a huge garden city; coming from Tokyo, Berlin is a garden city. Even with the highly populated areas in the east, there's a hope, a huge green garden city. But coming back to the general tendency which Jacques Derrida mentioned, well, given the added benefit of support, electronic communication, technology. Is the city now resolving into a kind of globe covered with an electronic web of telecommunication, or is it resisting this tendency? I think this problem is closely linked to the double-binding task which you mentioned. You talked about the tendency to turn this city into a glorified network, but are there some remnants that have something to do with the historical destiny of this city?

DERRIDA: Well, that's a huge question. In answer to such a question I would suggest that if there is a problem of the city, any city for example, it's to the extent that there is some resistance to the electronic level of the identity of the place. If there

were no resistance, you don't need any more planning for any city. The city would be simply a reminder of the past, an archive, that's all. It's only because there is a struggle between a desire for the place, for vocation, for visibility, for belonging. Although belonging is impossible to define, it's a paradoxical structure. Nevertheless, there is an indestructible, irresistible desire for belonging, for a place, for appropriation, for property etc, and this desire is resisting the electronic globalisation which is also another manifestation of the same desire. You cannot simply oppose a non-desire on the side of electronic globalisation and a desire for belonging. An electronic dissolution and everything in association with it, telecommunication etc, is also an extension of this same desire with new forms and new mentalities, less and less immediately mastered. It's not simply opposition – even the concept of resistance will have to be re-elaborated because it's not a resistance from something to something absolutely diverse. It's a resistance within the same desire which is not in and of itself. Desire is not in and of itself, the way of belonging is not in and of itself; and this leads us back again to this question of foundation. When I said that there was no such thing as self-foundation, it was not only abstractly philosophical. For instance, who will decide about the refoundation of Berlin? Apparently, the administration of Berlin, but we know already that the state will ultimately intervene in everything which will be done in Berlin because in 12 years it will be the capital of Germany. But as you know, even the German state will

decide by itself. The German State will decide everything in terms of money, investment, organisation and it will decide about it under the pressure of the European community.

FORSTER: One could of course, and I think it's very helpful, recognise the extent to which these divisions which would allow one to talk about the formation of this solution of cities. City as opposed to country dwellers let's say, have long been transcended. Even the person equipped with a car-phone is extending a living room situation or an office situation to the inter-spaces which would have separated the private sphere from the professional sphere. The typical city dweller is an apartment dweller, and to that extent s/he has no longer all this constant aperture back to an identity between land, real estate and personality. S/he is always woven into a fabric that is the product of the civilisation which is represented by the city. In other words, the city dweller can retain the city dweller's status and mentality in the absence if the city. You can ship them out to Connecticut, but they will remain New Yorkers and act on the interest of New York in the legislature of Connecticut. The city dweller becomes an ancient independent dweller of the city as a physical location.

BOOKS

CHARLES RENNIE MACKINTOSH

CHARLES RENNIE MACKIN-TOSH at the Hunterian Art Gallery, *Glasgow, 1991, 55pp, colour ills, price N/A*
Reviewed by
GRAHAM OVENDEN

As the reprisal of man's relationship with the natural world gathers momentum, it would seem logical that the works of designers such as Charles Rennie Mackintosh should hold the seed of much which has been discovered for future generations.

Writing as primarily a 'Gothic' enthusiast I find much which gives complete satisfaction and fulfillment within the body of this great Scottish master's achievements. Certainly, Mackintosh's ability to juxtapose a severely geometric, even asymmetric geometry, with a particularly gratifying linear ornamentation, in its counterpose, shows a closeness to the Northern Gothic traditions. Moreover, it embodies an essential spirit which unifies the seemingly disparate parts into an organic whole. This must surely place him within the aspirations of the Medieval and Celtic traditions.

The breaking of a wall surface into linear verticality, whether structural or ornamental, and the elongation of figurative forms which seem to possess substance above mere decoration, again gives the sense of an integrated purpose which looks both to the past, and this writer would hope, the future also.

Equally, within his furniture design, one is primarily aware of what is the burgeoning pantheistic nature of Mackintosh's conceptions. For example, the hall chair designed in 1901 for Windyhill has a physical presence reminiscent of the stone seats on which the representatives of a deity took office. To achieve such monumentality in wood is no mere accident, for Mackintosh's intuitive understanding of strength, tempered by a sense of formal 'rightness', amounts to genius. As with the linear arias of certain great musicians whose works one feels to have always existed, once having seen and understood the fulfillment of Mackintosh's designs, it is almost impossible to conceive of their non-existence.

Particularly satisfying are the complete conceptions with which Mackintosh and his ilk have evolved. In the present when, either due to insufficient will or to the moment's fashion, the majority of architectural projects seem skimped in detail, or even worse, arbitrary in the placement of artifacts within, Mackintosh not only delights, excites, but most profoundly of all, satisfies both the intellect and the sensual . . . his work is wholesome in every sense of the meaning.

Even in later Mackintosh, such as the guest bedroom at Derngate, in which he skillfully plays with pure geometry, one is still aware of the organic process of nature; growth has been reduced to geometric symbolism of the severest simplicity but the thrusting verticality leads to the spreading canopy. There remains an underlying affinity of sentiment with living matter.

The French architect Mallet Stephens may well declaim 'If I were God, I should design like Mackintosh!' Well, yes, but I suspect the older primeval god, Pan, is more the motivation for his genius.

'Charles Rennie Mackintosh at the Hunterian Gallery' proves a valuable introduction to the works of both Charles and Margaret Mackintosh. All aspects of their original genius are dealt with and their imagery is proven both sensitive and powerful. Their creative draughtsmanship and innate ability to infuse the most modest work with a strong validity is a lesson for students. In this age of 'specialisation' I wonder how many of our 'heroes' are able to encompass both graphic representation and the concrete form with equal virtuosity? The open-minded student may learn much of process and integrity from their example, and this little volume may be of pleasure to many, and an instructive example to the judicious.

Design for mural decoration, Buchanan Street Tea Rooms, Glasgow 1896

ANTEBELLUM ARCHITECTURE OF KENTUCKY

by Clay Lancaster, University Press of Kentucky, 1991, 338pp, b/w ills, HB $50

The distinctive regional architecture of Kentucky has been analysed in this book by Clay Lancaster. He illustrates the range of stylistic development using historical background, drawings, photographs and floorplans, showing both features and detail.

Among the buildings discussed are those by well-known early American architects such as Benjamin Henry Latrobe and Thomas Jefferson. Lancaster also pays special attention to the Geometric Style which produced many notable Kentucky monuments. This book embraces a broad scope by showing how the architecture that resulted from Kentucky's fertile eclecticism constitutes a rich and rewarding architectural heritage.

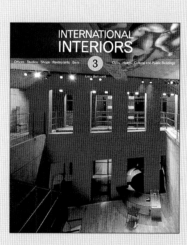

INTERNATIONAL INTERIORS

by Lucy Bullivant, Thames and Hudson, London, 1991, 256pp, ills, HB £42

This is a comprehensive biennial survey of new public design, providing designers with a rich but compact source of information on materials and ideas.

This third volume includes offices, cultural buildings, fashion shops, hotels, bars and restaurants from Japan, USA, Germany, Britain and Australia. Each project is fully illustrated with colour photographs, the architect's plans and drawings and an accompanying critical commentary.

THE SELF BUILD BOOK: How to Enjoy Designing and Building Your Own Home

by Jon Broome and Brian Richardson, Green Books, Bideford, Devon, 1991, 253pp, b/w ills, PB £15

The Self-Build Book gives both inspiration and practical information to those who want to build their own house. It gives a clear and lucid explanation of a variety of techniques of building including the method that Walter Segal evolved.

The book is divided into five parts. In the first, the authors describe their own experience of self-build and outline some of the ideas involved in designing one's own house. Two sources of inspiration, Walter Segal, who initiated the Lewisham self-build project and Christopher Alexander, author of *The Timeless Way of Building* and *A Pattern Language* are introduced here. Part four is a complete account of the Segal method of timber construction and includes basic step-by-step instructions on how to build a Segal house.

Part three covers the practical and financial side of a self-build enterprise and the final part analyses the potential role of self-build in the present housing situation.

LE NOUVEAU DESIGN ITALIEN

by Nally Benati, Terrail, Paris, 1991, 223pp, ills, price N/A

54 young Italian artists showcase their work in this French language book. Work includes furniture, lighting, interiors and graphics and the styles range from Hi-tech, Classical and Post-Modern. Alberto Alessi introduces this eclectic collection.

TWENTIETH CENTURY DESIGN CLASSICS: From the Anglepoise Lamp to the Zippo Lighter

by Chris Pearce, Green Wood, London, 1991, 128pp, ills, HB £14.95

A wide ranging pictorial review of the century's most popular and enduring styles covering architecture,

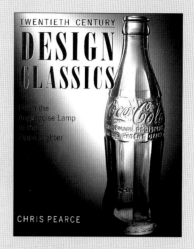

cars, cigarette packets, furniture and trademarks.

Chris Pearce, a design consultant and social historian has included popular icons from both Europe and the United States. British Classics include Penguin Books (Edward Young 1935), the Aga Stove (Douglas Scott 1938) and London Transport which under the directorship of Frank Pick in 1933 became a patron of Modern architecture (eg Arnos Grove Station by Charles Holden), graphics (The Underground Map designed by Beck) and industrial design (The Routemaster 1954 by Scott and Ottoway). American design classics include the Coca-Cola bottle, the McDonald's Logo, the Jeep and Lucky Strike Cigarette Packet.

DESIGN JURIES ON TRIAL: THE RENAISSANCE OF THE DESIGN STUDIO

by Kathryn H Anthony, Van Nostrand Reinhold, New York, 1992, 257pp, ills, price N/A

Design Juries on Trial unlocks the door to the mysterious design jury system, exposing its hidden agendas and helping you overcome intimidation, confrontation, and frustration. It explains how to improve the success rate of submissions to juries and how to reconstruct the jury system in education and professional practice. Those who shape design decisions are sure to benefit from this resource.

Guidelines are put forward that are based on extensive research made during a seven-year period, carried out through systematic observations and videotape recordings of design students, educators and practitioners. Interviews with architects such as Richard Meier, Peter Eisenman, Cesar Pelli and Robert AM Stern are featured.

BOOKS

EXQUISITE CORPSE

EXQUISITE CORPSE: WRITING ON BUILDINGS
by Michael Sorkin, Verso, London, 1991, 365pp, HB £19.95

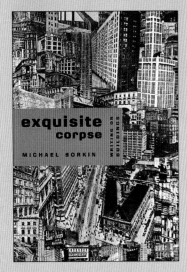

We here reproduce the author's Introduction from his volume of essays, with a commentary by **Charles Jencks**

Architectural critics of a highly critical disposition come in four main types: the hit-and-run expert who writes weekly columns and moves on quickly to his next victim; the jealous husband who works on his audience's love of gossip, intrigue and envy: the Byzantine conspiracy theorist who takes 30 years of research to find that Gothic Architecture was really created by the lost tribe of Germanica; and the street-smart surgeon who cuts up his victims with such relish that they sometimes enjoy it. Deyan Sudjic is an example of the first, Martin Pawley the second, Anthony Vidler the third and Michael Sorkin the fourth. Diane Ghirardo combines the second and third types; the anonymous *Pilotis, Sour Grapes*, and *Astragal* run amok all over the fourth.

Michael Sorkin, who studied at the AA and has been an architectural critic for the *Village Voice* for ten years, obviously intends his work to be judged as architectural journalism, not criticism; the quick kill rather than the considered judgement. This explains why he will sometimes assassinate in preference to analysing. Paul Goldberger, architectural critic of the *NY Times*, is axed as 'the Number One Toady' Why? Because of his continuous support of Philip Johnson. The latter's AT&T?: 'Not to put too fine a point on it , the building sucks.' Not to put too fine a point on this, frustrated Modern architects in New York love such barbs. Perhaps surprisingly these cracks put Sorkin in the same boat as Johnson and Goldberger – fundamental stylists promoting their ideologies. Right versus left politics now become sublimated by the Style Wars; no wonder the protagonists secretly admire each other. Their 'diatribes and encomiums' as Sorkin calls his hit-jobs and cheerleading, interlock and legitimate those of his enemies.

So read Sorkin's collection *Exquisite Corpse* with the ironic enjoyment it deserves, realising that his soi-disant philosophy goes not much further than the effusions of a New Age Technofantast who wants to 'recuperate dreamy science' and re-establish a romantic modernism. His position is not what counts: rather it is his street-smart voice and insights into the Style-Wars, its 'cabal and power trips', its endless self-promotion and hype. For presenting these with wit, however nasty we – as Johnson and Goldfinger – can be grateful. *CJ*

Introduction
by Michael Sorkin

When I was in architectural school in the early 70s, it seemed almost impossible to practice architecture. Building was so bound up with structures of power, the only responsible thing, I thought, was to resist; to be something other than the wagging tail of the Yankee dog. I turned to writing as the extension of architecture by other means, trying to make a space in which I could practice. I never saw myself as an architectural writer but as an architect for whom writing was an additional, necessary medium. If the work has tended to divide itself largely into panegyrics and polemics, it's because big issues were at stake.

A deep love of modern architecture has been the centre for me: I grew up on modernism which always seemed to harbour both adventure and hope. When I started writing, however, modern architecture was beleaguered. By the 70s, conventional wisdom was that modernism was a burned-out monolith; that penal-style housing projects, antiseptic glass slabs and dead cities were its inevitable issue. This insistent reading had many sorry consequences. To begin, the link between modern architecture and failed social policy was used as a lever to discredit the idea of architecture's engagement with social activism, a modernist bedrock. The past two decades in the US have produced an architectural culture preoccupied with empty style, acquiescent in trivialising the full constructive scope of architecture's possibility. It seems, sometimes, to have been non-stop lifestyles of the rich and famous, all beach houses and Disneyland.

An ironic corollary of this obsessive style-mongering (so in tune with the larger culture of yuppification and Reaganism) was to obscure the actual diversity of modernist expression. Modern architecture had been so thoroughly identified with anti-style, its geniuses – El Lissitzky, Niemeyer, de Klerk, Scharoun, Candela, Lautner, Golf, even Wright – became virtual non-persons. Although post-modernism arrived riding the nag of history, its view was blinkered, its horizons hemmed by the Villa Giulia and Monticello. That architectural culture at the end of the 20th century should be dominated by apostles of 'classicism,' however ersatz can only be the symptom of an institution in deep distress, a vile zit on the schnozz of culture.

Not that modern architecture was blameless. In its own internal wars, functionalism – that moralising discourse of effects – vanquished all comers. Like much of modern art and architecture, this asymptotic discourse tended to an impoverished, minimalist condition, hubristically muddled about chicken and egg. The bad message of functionalism was simply that every element in a building had to give an account of itself in terms of a limited range of uses, expunging pleasure, whimsy, joy or happy irrationality. Cloddish neo-con reaction to modernism's failures of argument has lead to the present crisis of authority and the dumb exultation of the historic, the last refuge of banality. This has yielded truly freakish results: an orgy of solipsism, narcissist architecture, absorbed with self-reference and facade.

A willingness to look outside of architecture for invigoration is one of modernism's happiest proclivities. Functionalism's historic affinity was for technology, and modern architecture has been deservedly bopped for a certain servility before the machine. It is, after all, a small stretch for the mechanical – a logical (and inevitable) terrain for architectural invention – to lapse into the mechanistic; for technology to seem oppressive and autonomous. While the logics of mass-production are still intermittently introduced as potentially redemptive (an old trope), the products are, with few exceptions, dreary, alienating and uneconomic: a Taylorised equality of deprivation; back to the USSR. But, whatever the successes and failures of factory production as a solution to the housing question, locating science only here has served to de-poeticise the architectural act. For me, always fascinated by big technology (my architectural formation was *inter alia* at the time of the moon shots) and its scintillating relation to architecture, tech's co-optation by the Pentagon and Detroit was another reason for dismay. The recuperation of dreamy science for architecture has been a high hope for me.

The biggest baby chucked out with the functionalist bathwater, however, was the prospect of an inventive urbanism. The very idea of city planning had been made disreputable by post-war experience and its two spectacularly failed models: urban renewal and the suburbs. Physical planning is still flinching from the disrepute of this love-enslavement to social engineering, and had been almost entirely abandoned as a municipal function in the United States; the public realm reduced to reacting to the shoves and slaps of the invisible hand. A clear result of this paranoid fear of innovation has been the elevation of nominally historic forms to the status of the only complicit possibilities for the new. In Manhattan – to cite only the example closest to hand – the route of Disneyfication, the projection of a muzzy and spurious past authenticated by putative links to local tradition is the dominant paradigm. From the phony carnivalesque of the South Street Seaport, to the veneered festivity of the new Times Square, to the anorexic vision of Battery Park City, we're awash in trumped (often Trumped-)up history. Absent any other municipal imagination, the Landmarks Preservation Commission has symptomatically risen to the status of planning agency, empowered just to say no.

New York has been at the centre of my writing activities and I'm beholden to the *Village Voice*, which has been my primary journalistic venue. However, this connection impelled a certain direction: as a leftish New Yorker writing for a leftish New York weekly I've felt obliged to write mainly about New York. And – aside from the scintillating world-large parochialisms of local architectural politics – New York had only one real story in the Reagan/Koch years:

Who profits? In a deregulated climate in which planning had devolved into a series of give-away strategics for stimulating 'development,' writing about architectural expression often seemed not simply irrelevant but complicit with the occlusive needs of capital. Their own fascinations notwithstanding, questions of style are simply peripheral to these issues: for the woman staring at the CRT screen in the windowless back office, whether the doo-dads on the roof are Tuscan or De-Con will be of no great import. To paraphrase a dimly remembered line from somewhere in Marx, 'never mind the fluctuations in the price of beef, the sacrifice remains constant for the ox.'

As chronicler of the price of New York architectural beef, I found myself consistently confronted by two striking absences. The first is the almost complete lack of serious building. Although New York City holds a breathtaking concentration of architectural talent, the last 20 years have seen not one great new work of architecture in the city. Our mode of architectural production has become so rationalized, and architectural patronage so myopic, that the hopes of our best reside in Tokyo or Los Angeles – anywhere but here. Indeed, the dizzying rise of the gallery and exhibition scene, if mainly due to the supply-side spiral of the 80s art market, is surely also a signifier of no alternative for those who would experiment or dream.

The second void is that of criticism itself. Although there has surely been a sharp increase in the number of people writing about architecture and an increase in the sophistication of academic writing, the quality of architectural journalism remains dismal. In part, this is a product of the long wave in architectural construction.

Unlike other journalistic criticism, the function of architectural writing in relation to the seismograph of the market is not so direct, making the brisk commerce of overnight valorisation dodgier. Absent such visible consequences for advertising revenue, most papers and general interest publications have little use for architecture. Although New York produces more such writing than most towns, this work scores very low on the acuity meter; mainly the higher publicity, drumbeating for development or hawking this week's fashion.

As suggested earlier, my work has mainly tended to fall into diatribes and encomiums. I have always had, shall we say, a certain penchant for invective; always thought my aim truer from the hip. Certainly, writing about culture in the Reagan era offered endless inducements to reach for my revolver. For this I have no regrets. My critical purposes are polemical and the situation in New York has been mainly bleak. If I have often focused on architecture's institutional culture, on critics, cabals, and power trips, it is not simply because these tempests have gathered wind in a city which has forsaken a real building culture but because these debates are agenda setters of global ramification. My Phillippics (you know who I mean) have been frequent because a critic's torpedo must home on power and its symbols. More, as an architect looking for the space of a joyful practice, these were the roadhogs blocking the way for me and many I admire.

This book, then, is a kind of envoi, an adieu to the journalistic trenches as I return at last to a more full time architectural practice. I've chosen 50-odd pieces (winnowing is a painful trial – the infelicities that jump from the page! – the zingers

forsaken!) from the past ten years which are, I think, representative. They appear as they appeared, in chronological order, rather then in terms of some taxonomy of coherence that never was. If, however, I might single out a lone thread, it is the celebration and defence of the repressed discourses of modernism –the technical, the social, the fantastic, the tectonic, the sensual – which flower again in the wake of the tattered hegemony of functionalist and historicist speech. My hope for post-functionalist architecture is not that it will be decoupled from an abiding sense of social purpose but that its agendas – political and artistic – will be both progressive and free; that the fun will get put back into functionalism. If these essays have in any way advanced these goals, they've served their purpose.

The title of the book celebrates one of the mightiest repressed discourses of them all. It's drawn from the famous collaborative folded paper game beloved of the Surrealists, described by Breton as capable of 'holding the critical intellect in abeyance and of fully liberating the mind's metaphorical activity.' Never mind that it's the greatest portmanteau metaphor for modern culture ever, demanding that its maddening, slipperyconcatenation somehow be read, it's also a perfect image of the city: our greatest, most out of control collective artifact. And it also seems to describe the somewhat aleatory basis for this collection.

Finally, to all of those who were kind enough to write over the years and to whom I never replied: thanks and forgive me. I dedicate this collection to you and to those anonymous friends who kept these articles circulating through the xerox ether of the architectural samizdat.

BACK ISSUES

ARCHITECTURAL DESIGN

Architectural Design continues its vigorous and wide-ranging treatment of architectural trends that have vital importance today. Improving its already high quality of reproduction and presentation, the magazine now has an enlarged format and a new, innovative design.

The six double issues published each year, are each devoted to a major theme of topical relevance.

Whilst having a pluralist approach, *Architectural Design* has not been afraid to focus in depth on specific directions and always reflects the contemporary in its assessment of architecture. The magazine specialises in publishing the work of international architects who are influential for their critical theories as well as their built work. The treatment of the divergent subjects examined over the years has had a profound impact on the architectural debate, making *AD* an invaluable record for architectural thinking, criticism and achievements.

Recent themes include *Paternoster Square, Free Space Architecture, Modern Pluralism, Berlin Tomorrow, A New Spirit in Architecture, New Museums, Deconstruction, Post-Modern Triumphs in London* and *Aspects of Modern Architecture*. Architects featured include Peter Cook, Peter Eisenman, Norman Foster, Zaha Hadid, Hans Hollein, Arata Isozaki, Leon Krier, Daniel Libeskind, Philippe Starck, James Stirling, Bernard Tschumi, Robert Venturi, Lebbeus Woods and many more. An additional magazine section focuses on the most stimulating exhibitions, books and criticism of the moment. Maintaining a high standard of writing and design, the magazine is extensively illustrated and includes articles and interviews by well-known architects and critics including Maxwell Hutchinson, Lucinda Lambton, Christopher Martin Ken Powell, Paul Johnson and Anthony Quiney.

SUBSCRIBE NOW AND START TO CREATE YOUR OWN ENCYCLOPEDIA OF INTERNATIONAL ARCHITECTURE IN THE MAKING

BOOKS

Une construction à Quebec: Maisons-Poteaux-Drapeaux, *installed on the Plains of Abraham, Quebec City, 1989 (from the exhibition* Territoires d'artistes: Paysages verticaux*) constructed by Melvin Charney, taken from* Parables and other Allegories, *a comprehensive record of the work of this architect/artist*

BOOKS RECEIVED:

PERSPECTIVE GRID SOURCE BOOK: Computor Generated Tracing Guides For Architectural and Interior Design Drawings *by Ernest Burden, Chapman and Hall, London, 1991, 190pp, Ills, PB £29*

PLANNING FOR CAD SYSTEMS *by Chris Austin, McGraw-Hill, Berkshire, 1991, 159pp b/w ills, HB £24.95*

DESIGN AND TECHNOLOGY IN ARCHITECTURE *revised edition by David Guise, Chapman and Hall, London, 1991, 297pp, b/w ills, PB £16.45*

HOME FRONT FURNITURE: British Utility Design 1941-51 *by Harriet Dover, Gower, Aldershot, 1991, 105pp, b/w ills, HB £30*

LOUIS I KAHN: In the Realm of Architecture by David B Brownlee and David G De Long, Rizzoli, New York, 1991, 448pp, PB price N/A

'His work has a presence, an aura, unmatched by that of any other architect of the present day. Far beyond even the works of Frank Lloyd Wright, Mies van der Rohe, and Le Corbusier, it is brooding, remote, mysterious' Vincent Scully writes. This monograph accompanies a major new retrospective of Kahn's work, organised by The Museum of Contemporary Art in Los Angeles, representing the culmination of ten years' work and allocated resources. As such it is one of the first fully comprehensive re-evaluations of the architecture of Louis I Kahn. Six essays make up the main body of critical text, preceded with an introduction by Vincent Scully. In addition a whole colour portfolio of photographs newly commissioned from Grant Muntford form an insert between the articles and individual project descriptions.

The exhibition's organisers venerate Kahn for his 'value and relevance' to the present as a designer and as an architectural thinker. It is for this reason that the six chapters which represent all six phases of his career combine chronology, typology and the architect's personal philosophy to give the complete spectrum of Kahn's extraordinary abilities and achievements. Similarly just the amount of visual material reveals Kahn's diversity. An array of drawings, sketches, paintings, scale models and archival photographs are interspersed with the main text.

Such is the scale and scope of this book that it will prove not only of great interest but invaluable to architects, historians as well as a broader audience.

FABRICS AND WALLPAPERS: Design Sources and Inspiration by Barty Philips, Ebury, London, 1991, 208pp, HB £25

This book provides a lively, authoritative and accessible record of early patterns. From Reveillon's beribboned and garlanded papers to the 1970's screen prints by Zandra Rhodes, this book offers a fascinating and detailed insight into the history of fabrics and wallpapers. It is illustrated throughout with specially commissioned colour photographs.

THE INTERIOR DIMENSION: A Theoretical Approach to Enclosed Space by Joy Monice Malnar and Frank Vodvarka, Van Nostrand Reinhold, New York, 1992, 365pp, price N/A

Traditionally, architectural theory has emphasised the exterior rather than the interior of buildings. This book, however, turns the approach inside out by viewing the interior as the designer's primary concern. An eclectic view is adopted as many disciplines are brought into play to produce a history of spatial design from the first century BC to the present day. Organised into three parts, this book forms a coherent whole avoiding historical linearity.

CLASSICAL
ARCHITECTURE

DEMETRI PORPHYRIOS

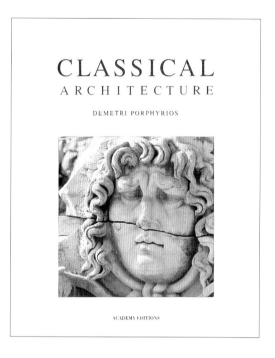

Demetri Porphyrios argues eloquently that 'architecture makes us see the building craft from which it is born, from which it detaches itself as art, and to which it always alludes.' In a series of tightly argued essays, the author discusses the role of imitation, tectonics, ornament and originality in architecture, showing that the classical is that which speaks of tradition always in a modern voice.

In the first chapter the author examines the theory of imitation, and the position it occupies in classical thought. The second is devoted to the significance of tectonics in architecture. The next chapter examines the relations between building and architecture and the way in which we may say that 'classicism is not a style'. The fourth chapter studies classical ornament and the role it plays in architecture. The fifth chapter addresses the principles of the traditional city and makes the claim for revitalising common sense. Finally, in the sixth chapter, the author looks at what tradition really means and how it relates to modernity.

'A work is classical not because it is immutable, eternal and sacred but because it continually searches for and brings out the new.' *Classical Architecture* is both a pedagogic and critical book; it has implications for our present-day theory of style, our view of history, and for the practice of architecture. Lavishly illustrated in colour, *Classical Architecture* is an invaluable book for readers from a wide range of disciplines and anyone who cares about the place of architecture in modern life.

305 x 252mm, 200 pages, over 300 illustrations mostly in colour
ISBN: 0 85670 969 0 Hardback £35.00
Available from good bookstores worldwide

ACADEMY EDITIONS • LONDON
42 Leinster Gardens London W2 3AN Tel: 071 402 2141

BOOKS

BOOKS RECEIVED:

THE DIRECTORY OF PRODUCTS AND SERVICES for Museums, Galleries, Historic Houses, Heritage and Related arts organisations *by Maggie Heath, The Museum Development Company, 1991, 520pp, PB £29.95*

INTERIOR DESIGN OF THE ELECTRONIC OFFICE: The Comfort and Productivity Payoff *by Walter B Kleeman Jnr, Chapman and Hall, London, 1991, 294pp, b/w ills, PB price N/A*

WILLEM JAN NEUTELINGS ARCHITECT *Stichting Rotterdam – Maaskant Foundation, Uitgeverij 010 Publishers, Rotterdam, 1991, 60pp, colour ills, PB price N/A*

RENDERING THE VISUAL FIELD: ILLUSION BECOMES REALITY *by Kevin Forseth, Chapman and Hall, London, 1991, 160pp, b/w ills, PB price N/A*

CHARACTER TRADEMARKS *by John Mendenhall, Angus and Robertson, London, 1991, 132pp, colour ills, PB £10.95*

FIFTY YEARS OF NATIONAL BUILDINGS RECORD 1911-1991 *by the Royal Commission on the Historical Monuments of England. Introduction by Sir John Summerson, Trigon Press, Beckenham, 1991, 68pp, b/w ills, HB £14.95*

FAITH IN ESTATES – COUNCIL TENANTS AND THEIR HOUSING *An assessment of housing estates in Kirklees and Lewisham, The Prince's Trust and the Royal Jubilee Trusts, London, 1991, 142pp, b/w ills, PB £5.00*

PAY NOW OR PAY LATER *by the National Research Council, National Academy Press, Washington DC, 1991, 54pp, b/w ills, PB £16.45*

DESIGN AND TECHNOLOGY IN ARCHITECTURE *revised edition by David Guise, Chapman and Hall, London, 1991, 297pp, b/w ills, PB £19.50*

HELLENISTIC SCULPTURE

by R Smith, Thames and Hudson, London, 1991, 287pp, b/w ills, PB £6.95

The exuberant realism and virtuoso technique of Hellenistic sculpture formed the basis of much later European Art. Under Alexander and his cosmopolitan successors, sculptors enriched the classical Greek repertoire with a whole range of new subjects – hermaphrodites, putti, peasants, boxers – and new styles – baroque treatment, genre figures, individualised portraiture. Professor Smith offers a reappraisal of this entire artistic epoch as a period of innovation, demonstrating the variety, subtlety and complexity of its styles. Numerous illustrations reveal the skill and inventiveness of the Hellenistic masters, who created works of great beauty and expressive power. The result is a lively survey of a vital phase in the evolution of Western art.

COLOR CONSULTING: A Survey of International Color Design

by Harold Linton, Chapman and Hall, London, 1991, 196pp, colour ills, HB £43.50

ETTORE SOTTSASS

by Jan Burney, Trefoil Publications, London, 1991, 192pp, b/w ills, HB price N/A

The architect and designer Ettore Sottsass encapsulates the Italian achievement in design since the Second World War. Like so many of his contemporaries in design, he trained as an architect, and in the early 1950s several of his INA Casa housing projects were built. But he has practised mainly as a designer. His career also highlights the connection between design and industry in Italy: his work for Olivetti is legendary, for example, and covers

early electronic computers, typewriters and video terminals, office systems and seating. In 1980 Sottsass broke away from the classical modern design he had developed for his corporate customers into a range of daring post modern designs under the Memphis group label. Their use of harsh colours and unusual shapes brought the work immediate attention, and Ettore Sottsass remains a force in the international world of product design. This book examines the paradoxes and contradictions of his career, in particular how his own upbringing and his political convictions have shaped his view of design as a social and human activity.

THE ELECTRONIC DESIGN STUDIO: Architectural Knowledge and Media in the Computer Era

edited by Malcolm McCullough, William J Mitchell, and Patrick Purcell, MIT Press, Cambridge, Mass, 1990, 505pp, b/w ills, HB £44.95

ARCHITECTURE FROM WITHOUT – Theoretical Framings for a Critical Practice

by Diana I Agrest, MIT Press, Cambridge, Mass, 1991, over 200pp, HB $40.50

'It is from the city (the unconscious of architecture), from outside, that critical work on architecture is developed' Diana Agrest writes. In this book she explores the symbolic dimension of architecture from the perspective of the modern city through a remarkable range of subjects – the relationship between architectural and urban ideologies, the symbolic performance of architecture in relation to the urban condition, the formal and ideological development of a building type, the relationship between architecture and other visual discourses, and the position of gender and body in Western architecture. Agrest focuses on the urban condition of architecture as a possibility for rethinking its own limits. Her understanding of architecture as ideology from perspective of signification and culture opens up the question of the specificity of the architectural, unmasking functional determinism.

The work of Diana Agrest, developed in teaching, writing and practice, is an important contribution to the architectural discourse of the past two decades.

SIGN DESIGN by Mitzi Sims, Thames and Hudson, 1991, 176pp, colour ills, PB £16.95

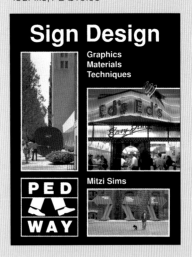

Beginning with a survey of the types and uses of signs, the author guides the reader through the design process, from the initial briefing to the installation of the final product and offers the designer all the information needed to make practical creative decisions. This book provides an invaluable source of reference and inspiration.

FRANK LLOYD WRIGHT

THOMAS A HEINZ

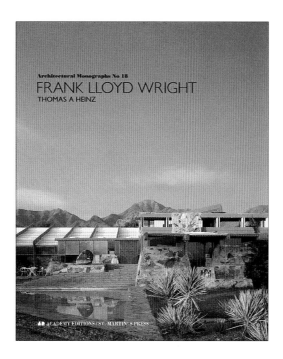

In a major new contribution on the work of this iconoclastic and flamboyant architect, who is widely regarded as the greatest that America has ever produced, Thomas A Heinz – both an architect and writer – uses his extensive experience in the restoration of Frank Lloyd Wright buildings to present aspects of them that have previously gone unnoticed. Concentrating primarily on residences, the author uses his own photographs to examine construction techniques that are just as unorthodox as the architect himself, showing that Wright's approach to detailing was pragmatic, rather than conventional, and was based on traditional common sense.

As Heinz writes in his introductory essay to this pictorial survey, 'Frank Lloyd Wright's buildings are not just differently designed, they are differently constructed. Wright had to invent or re-invent many items and systems to bring about his new art. Every design, every hidden detail, is evidence of Wright's unique intelligence . . . Other architects who designed in the Wrightian mode often were more consistent than the one who originated the style, and, in fact, some of their creations are more apt to appear as the quintessential Prairie House than are many of Wright's, with his little quirks and exceptions.'

Frank Lloyd Wright's concepts invariably incorporated all spatial elements, such as furniture and decoration, into his idea of 'total design'. Thomas A Heinz photographed Wright interiors while they were still intact, prior to items being sold in the recent frenzy for anything that he has produced, thus providing valuable historical documentation for students of his work.

305 x 252mm, 144 pages, extensively illustrated in colour
ISBN: 1 85490 110 9 Hardback £19.95 Paperback £14.95
Available from good bookstores worldwide

ACADEMY EDITIONS • LONDON
42 Leinster Gardens London W2 3AN Tel: 071 402 2141

CHRISTOPHER MARTIN
TALKING ABOUT TELEVISION

People who make television arts programmes sometimes like to get away from actually doing it and – presuming that some generous patron is paying for the enterprise and assuming that the circumstances of the forum are adequately lavish – are happy to spend a weekend or so discussing the various ways they manifest their genius and grumbling about the appalling (and unappreciated by the public) difficulties, economic or political, that constrain them.

I once attended an agreeably luxurious seminar (paid for by Walter Annenburg) in a ranch at Palm Springs, California. Television people from England and America had been invited to discuss the future of arts programmes; how they were done in Britain and how the relatively arid television culture of America, as we grandly assumed it to be, might be irrigated by our example and strengthened by our advice. The proceedings would be taped. The transcript published. Our conclusions would cause the great edifice of American TV to tremble.

For days we talked. The tape recorders whirred on.

Sensibly, when we returned to Britain we forgot all about it. But some time later I was in Los Angeles and I enquired as to whether or not our deliberations had been of any value. As I had suspected the great weight of recorded conversation had proved too daunting to transcribe, let alone publish. Our aperçus were too evanescent. The mood of collective self-congratulation that we had generated may not, on playback, be very attractive. The mission was abandoned. The mighty American networks remained ignorant of our insights.

In those days such meetings always seemed to have an unreal, academic air to them. But nowadays there is a much less languid spirit abroad in discussions about the place of art on television.

On a hill outside Geneva there are a number of buildings which hold lofty, international meetings. At the top of the hill is the HQ of the European Broadcasting Union. The EBU runs an efficient secretariat and to Geneva come delegates – usually but not always TV bureaucrats – from the public service broadcasting companies of the continent (and sometimes America) to discuss common problems and, insofar as it is possible in Geneva, have a good time.

Thither this winter came the EBU's dauntingly entitled Arts Experts Group. The 'Experts' came from as far away as Helsinki and Portugal, Yugoslavia and Eire. Accoutred in the paraphernalia of simultaneous translation, sitting at desks covered with agendas and order papers, it was not difficult for the delegates to feel that they were participating in some great international event and that their deliberations might be of significance and importance.

In fact, as they well know, the EBU's cultural heart lies less in art than in sport and The Eurovision Song Contest. And so, by and large, it is in their home countries. The 'Experts' observe, with melancholy fortitude, a common phenomenon. All over Europe, all over the world, the squeeze is being put on public service broadcasting and in most cases the pips that are squeaking most are arts programmes. The BBC is not the only country reeling from the convulsions imposed on it by economic necessity and political pressure. France's non-commercial channel has been in a constant and hectic process of reorganisation for years. The arts have all but vanished from the main channels.

Belgium, the Scandinavian countries, Spain and Italy grow ever more incapable of planning any kind of future, so destructive are the pressures upon them. One United Kingdom delegate lost his reason for being in Geneva when the franchise of the company he represented was lost to a competitor.

Political pressures vary from country to country but the biggest, most inexorable force at work on the broadcasters is poverty. Alarmed managements are not seeking salvation through pouring money into arts programmes; budgets, already slender are being cut back further. The slots in which arts programmes have traditionally found a grudging home, be they never so late at night, are pushed ever later. Thus viewing figures, already small, dwindle into near invisibility. And that, of course, intensifies the conviction of management that these programmes have no following, and so no *raison d'être,* and therefore should be cut altogether. Many of the speakers complained that it was in vain for arts producers to claim that television was the conduit through which most people in Europe acquired much of their knowledge and understanding of art and culture. This was in marked contrast, they wryly observed, to the print media where there had been an absolute explosion of interest in the arts – to the point of surfeit.

So who is getting all the money that might, delegates wistfully hoped, be spent on programmes about art, architecture and design? Well, drama and light entertainment are the traditional big spenders and with the huge audiences they attract they are going to go on being so.

And then there is News.

Some speakers present at Geneva felt that News is taking over the world. Admittedly News had got more and more interesting in recent years. There had been the collapse of the Iron Curtain, the emergence of the free states of the former Soviet empire, there were the Israel-Arab peace talks, there were the hostages, there was the Gulf War. There was no questioning the fact that News was extremely absorbing at the moment and had become the back-bone of television. There was no question too that News was ferociously expensive to cover.

Nor could everything be blamed on the insensitivity to higher things of television's higher management. Delegates sadly observed that the very constituency for which they laboured – those people who read books, go to art galleries and concerts, visit old houses, cinemas and the theatre every so often – don't show as much relish for what the arts programme-makers offered them. In fact, television was something that didn't impinge much on their lives. They certainly didn't mind being on it once in a while and they were more than happy to share their views as to why arts programmes were so bad, but that was about it. A research study commissioned by ZDF in Germany had revealed that the audience for arts programmes in Europe was shrinking, was middle-aged, lived outside the great metropolitan, cultural centres, and was, the meeting seemed to think, rather a boring lot; unworthy of their efforts.

Charitably, the speakers seemed to assume that the short-comings of the programmes and their own failure to find the right tone of voice to communicate the message of the contemporary arts were the problem. But in fact, easy communication about so much of what goes on in the world of art nowadays is rendered almost impossible by the nature of what is being communicated; by what Sir Hugh Casson recently described as the 'ruthless obscurity' of so much modern art. He likened it to 'a party to which we haven't been invited'. Artists only have the right to be obscure, he said quoting Bertrand Russell, when they have demonstrated their ability to be clear. Instead, too often, they were 'narcissistic and vain. The whole world of art was degraded'.

At Geneva, however, the programme-makers seemed happy to take the blame themselves. Furthermore the delegates had taken measures to stem the tide. These they wanted to share with their European counterparts as well as finding out how the others were doing in the battle with the philistines.

Many countries, too many countries, put their money or what was left of it, into trying to make what seemed uncongenial to the viewer less so through the use of supposedly avant-garde techniques. They relied on fast-paced shenanigans with electronic graphics, zappy editing and a general emphasis on 'style' and 'presentation'.

Some of the stations, who could afford it, kept up the relentless pace all through the programme; laying a pounding musical sound-track with nervous over-editing, on shorter and shorter items.

Denmark, however, advocated the not very novel idea that the indifferent would only be lured into the pastures of truth and beauty by a famous figure. They proposed a series, which the EBU might consider, where artists would talk to television personalities about the mysteries of their craft, in their kitchens as they prepared for dinner.

Others showed rather more imagination and revealed rather more of their national identity. Yugoslavia, who before the civil war made attendance at Geneva a low priority, was wont at these meetings to show Belgrade's idea of the avant-garde (where it has recently been rediscovered) and experimental programme making. For jaded viewers from the decadent west of Europe these seemed blissfully old-fashioned – like excerpts from hitherto missing German Expressionist films of the 30s.

Finland which is not rich, as their representative acknowledged, in internationally famous artists at the moment, had put a large amount of its annual budget into a film on one artist who they had been assured was famous everywhere and who does certainly have a kind of international 'reclame' – Tom of Finland. Tom of Finland was a new one to me, then, but the amount of press coverage following his death a day or so after the gathering in Geneva had closed suggests that the people in Helsinki knew what they were doing. Tom of Finland was *the* artist of the leather-clad young male grinning and strutting in various erotic – depending on your point of view – poses. Whether he was the progenitor of the type or its apotheosis the film left unclear. But that was about all that was unclear in the movie. 'Are you actually going to transmit that stuff?' enquired the other delegates interestedly. Well, the man from Finland agreed, even in liberal Scandinavia the post-AIDS mood was not quite as liberal as it once had been; and the lateness of the transmission hour had its compensations. International sales were not expected to be heavy.

The assembly seemed divided by those who would go cheerfully down market and those who would give the audience, not so much what it wanted, but what it might like rather more. Thus, instead of making films about Rembrandt you made films about the people who collect Rembrandts – or forge them or steal them. If that didn't do the trick you could make films about 'style', about advertising icons, about cars, boots, faded pop-groups, kettles.

In this the delegates were sounding an overture to a debate which was then rumbling but has since erupted in Britain. It focuses on such areas as the output of Channel 4 from which much was expected in the way of cultural programmes. But Channel 4 has just run some particularly witless shows in what is dimly discernible as being an arts slot in which trendy, knowing film-makers and presenters share with the viewer their insights into such matters as hotels, Christmas presents, Jane Austen (how bad she is) and the Virgin Mary.

Many of British Television's problems are different from those of mainland Europe, but they are real enough. Some are self inflicted. In Britain it is almost a decade since substantial attention has been paid on television to what might be called the arts of the past – roughly speaking anything made or painted before Picasso. The fact has at last been noticed. There are plans afoot to have another look at an area now widely acknowledged to have been grossly neglected. Independent producers, seeking the patronage of the BBC, have been told that their chances will improve if they pay a little less attention to the 'style' that until recently seemed to be the key to success. What are wanted now are the old-fashioned virtues of clarity, accessibility and 'Authority'. The worry is that the golden thread that leads back to these things may have snapped. There's no Kenneth Clark to give his own patrician brand of *gravitas* to programmes. If there is, no-one seems to know about him. So next year a series by Kenneth Clark will be repeated.

It might be remarked that *Civilisation* was made and transmitted – very much against the grain of the times – in the late 60s. Popular and influential as it was, it was not necessarily acclaimed within the BBC. Young producers (of which I was one) thought it showed the right contemporary spirit to take exception to Clark's supposedly *de haut en bas* manner and expressed outrage at his 'un-progressive' views. Much more to our taste were the radical thunderings of John Berger that followed fairly hard upon *Civilisation* in *Ways of Seeing*. But unquestionably it is Clark who remains in the memory – perceptive, agreeably pessimistic, urbane. Berger seems lost in all the other rhetoric of the times.

The BBC is still very powerful. And a decent proportion of its relatively large income as well as its air time is given to arts programmes. That is not to say that everyone likes them or that they are all good. But there are undeniably a lot of them. In fact the arts have expanded during a time when the BBC is going through seismic change, which would have been unthinkable even a year or two ago. Perhaps the one most likely to affect the whole character of public service broadcasting in Britain is the decision to move from being a collegiate organisation making its own programmes to one more like a publishing house, commissioning but not necessarily producing many of its programmes. This is partly because of government legislation and a diminishing income, partly one suspects, because that is what the BBC wants to do itself. It is part of the commercial *zeitgeist*.

But the various acts of felo de se that the BBC has committed already seem a bit extreme, a response to Thatcherite pressures that no longer exist. And there is no confidence that the 'new' corporation will provide a framework in which programmes with the old Lord Clark kind of authority and confidence will flourish again.

BBC producers modestly allow that the high standards of their programmes owe something of their quality to the citadels of excellence in which they are made. It is the camaraderie of the cutting room, the standards of quality that are passed on from one camera crew to the next, the back-up, the training, the strength that comes from shared objectives that together have made the BBC famous – the envy of lesser lands. All this will shortly be in jeopardy.

Perhaps rather too much has been made of this. Citadels of excellence can also be towers of complacency. The much-vaunted *esprit de corps* can generate inward-looking complacency and narcissism. Outside producers reasonably claim that their standards are just as high and achieved at far less cost and with much less chest beating and vanity. But even the BBC's rivals are alarmed that too dramatic a change in the Corporation will damage the delicate ecology of broadcasting in the country – and thus the world.

So the largest as well as the smallest public service broadcasting authorities feel common threats. The problems are economic, political and endemic. It was in response to this that a meeting of the 'Arts Experts' had, on an earlier occasion in Germany, come up with a document rather grandly called 'The Mainz Manifesto'. The Manifesto went through much heart-searching, re-drafting and amendment in its making but looking at it now it seems better than anyone might have expected. It was addressed to the politicians who legislate for television as well as the bosses who run it. The signatories hoped that it would be read and discussed by the public. The Manifesto said things like:

Television is a critical part of our collective cultural memory. Its archives reflect the diversity and richness of all aspects of European life. We strongly believe that most Europeans do not want television to turn into the cultural equivalent of a theme park or a shopping mall. Television must continue to nourish all parts of human creativity to foster a culture that builds on and renews the past.

It is not too late to do what has to be done. A positive re-evaluation . . . by broadcasters of the importance of arts and culture in their schedules would be a clear signal that public service broadcasting is determined to stand up to steady erosion by commercial pressures . . . (they must) ensure cultural issues a continuing place on the agenda of mass communication.

The Manifesto was passed by the Experts and sent up to the more senior Programme Committee of the EBU for approval. Beyond that, it was hoped that it would go out, sanctified by the EBU imprimatur, to the Television Centres and Home Offices of the world. The Programme Committee, while not denying the Manifesto's argument, was alarmed at such eloquence. It refused to endorse it. Little has been heard of the Mainz Manifesto since then. But the issues it addressed have accumulated and grown more acute since it was written, and they are not going to go away.

AN EXAMPLE OF BRITISH TELEVISION'S ARTS COVERAGE IS CHANNEL 4'S 'WITHOUT WALLS' SERIES. ABOVE IS A STILL FROM 'THE TURNER PRIZE 1991', A PROGRAMME COVERING THE PRESENTATION OF THIS AWARD. NORMAN ROSENTHAL, HOWARD JACKOBSON, MARINA VAIZEY, NICHOLAS WARD-JACKSON, AND THE WINNER, ANISH KAPOOR, ARE SHOWN HERE DISCUSSING THE MERITS OF THE PRIZE

LEON KRIER

SOS VILLA SAVOYE

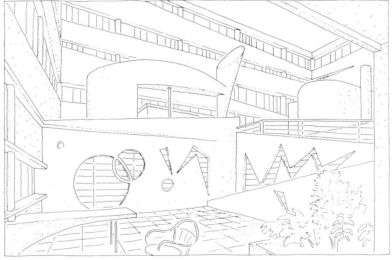

ABOVE: THE VILLA SAVOYE AS IT WAS ORIGINALLY COMPLETED; *BELOW*: CLEVER PEN-WORK ONLY THINLY DISGUISING THE
BRUTAL RAPE OF THE THREATENED WORLD CLASS MONUMENT

The modernist battlecry 'conservation has gone too far' seems finally to be calling home and striking at the heart of Modernism's most venerated and elegant shrine.

From painstaking description by our own informer at the Ministère de la Culture in Paris, our artist has been attempting to draw a realistic illustration of a project which, for obvious reasons, is kept under wraps because naked money interests are now threatening to engulf the Villa Savoye in Poissy in a pile of Scarpa cum Decon clichés. Apparently the master's very own foundation has, under pressure of its Japanese sponsors, given tacit agreement to a Hotel Development after having secured a reconstruction according to Corbu's plans at two-thirds scale in an amusement park along the A4 motorway.

Even though information has been confidentially circulating for several months, the scandal is raising more than a few eyebrows in the upper floors of the modernist camp. This however we feel is a unique occasion for conservationists and modernists to rally to a common cause.

So far it has sadly fallen upon arch-traditionalists like Culot, the Kriers, Porphyrios and apparently the Prince himself to be the lone protesters against an outrage of scandalous proportion. Is this not a tragic enough occasion for the modernists to swallow their pride, abandon an absurd dictum and at long last dare to save an object of beauty truly dear to their own heart?

Little can be expected from the International Conservation Lobby, firstly for obvious reasons and secondly because the universal reproach of being for ever backward-looking has turned many conservationists into ardent supporters of a form of architectural 'interventionism' of which the imminent Villa Savoye rape is but another example.

If you want to stop the massacre, support the campaign with your signature now. Write to SAVISA (Sauver la Villa Savoye) care of the Academy Group.

PATERNOSTER SQUARE
AND THE NEW CLASSICAL TRADITION

PATERNOSTER SQUARE, VIEW ACROSS LOWER COURT TOWARDS THE WEST, PAINTING BY EDWIN VENN

EDWIN VENN, PERSPECTIVE OF PATERNOSTER SQUARE FROM CHEAPSIDE

Architectural Design

Edited by Andreas C Papadakis

PATERNOSTER SQUARE
AND THE NEW CLASSICAL TRADITION

EDWIN VENN, PERSPECTIVE OF ST PAUL'S CHURCH YARD LOOKING WEST

ACADEMY EDITIONS • LONDON

Acknowledgements

We are grateful for the co-operation of Park Tower and Paternoster Associates in providing material for this issue, and in particular Keith Stone. Images for the Paternoster Square section provided by Park Tower unless otherwise stated. Other illustrations courtesy the architects.

Photographic Credits
p10: Guildhall Library, Corporation of London
p11: The Museum of London
p12: Aerofilms
p13: Guildhall Library
pp73-77: Nick Carter
pp92-93: Timothy Hursley

EDITOR
Dr Andreas C Papadakis

CONSULTANTS: Catherine Cooke, Terry Farrell, Kenneth Frampton, Charles Jencks
Heinrich Klotz, Leon Krier, Robert Maxwell, Demetri Porphyrios, Kenneth Powell, Colin Rowe, Derek Walker
EDITORIAL TEAM: Maggie Toy (House Editor), Richard Economakis, Vivian Constantinopoulos, Nicola Hodges, Helen Castle
DESIGN TEAM: Andrea Bettella (Senior Designer), Mario Bettella, Sharon Anthony, Owen Thomas
SUBSCRIPTIONS MANAGER: Mira Joka BUSINESS MANAGER: Sheila de Vallée

First published in Great Britain in 1992 by *Architectural Design* an imprint of the
ACADEMY GROUP LTD, 42 LEINSTER GARDENS, LONDON W2 3AN

ISBN: 1-85490-131-1 (UK)

Published in the United States of America by
ST MARTIN'S PRESS, 175 FIFTH AVENUE, NEW YORK, NY 10010
ISBN: 0-312-07931-1 (USA)

Printed and bound in Singapore

Contents

ARCHITECTURAL DESIGN PROFILE No 97

PATERNOSTER SQUARE
AND THE NEW CLASSICAL TRADITION

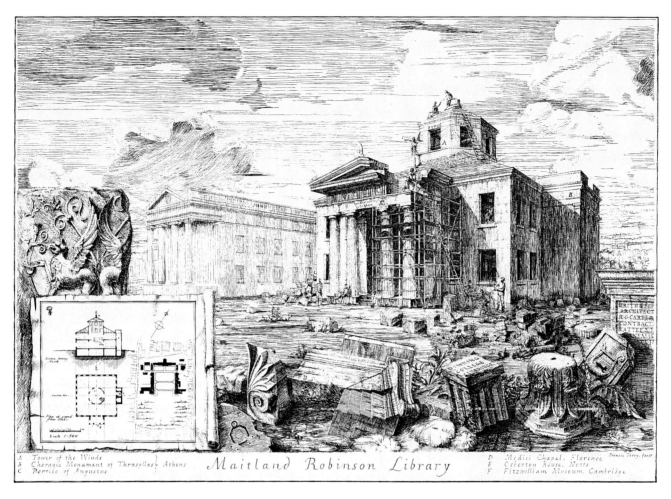

A — Tower of the Winds
B — Choragic Monument of Thrasyllas} Athens
C — Portico of Augustus

Maitland Robinson Library

D — Medici Chapel, Florence
E — Osterton House, Notts
F — Fitzwilliam Museum, Cambridge

Francis Terry, fecit

A — Ara Pacis, Rome
B — Magna Carter
C — Maison Carée, Nismes

The Drawing Rooms, 10 Downing Street.

G — Rose H — Daffodil J — Thistle K — Shamrock

D — Arch of Titus, Rome
E — Pellegrini Chapel, Verona
F — Thatcher in place of Apollo

Francis Terry, celt 1991

QUINLAN TERRY, MAITLAND ROBINSON LIBRARY AND DRAWING ROOMS AT 10 DOWNING STREET, LONDON

THE CLASSICAL REALITY

The Classical Revival in architecture began in earnest a decade ago. The first serious exhibition of Quinlan Terry's work (in 1981 at our own galleries) marked the start of what was to become a crusade to remake British architecture. There had, of course, been more senior traditionalist architects who survived the Modernist triumph of the post-war years and went on building in their own fashion. It mattered little to any of them that housing estates, shopping centres, City of London office blocks and comprehensive schools were designed in a manner which they found repugnant, derived from Le Corbusier, Mies, and Gropius. They had their clients – mostly a landed elite which scorned Modernism – and they could simply ignore the rest of the world.

They were an isolated minority, entirely marginal to the practice of architecture. An eminent figure in their ranks – for he appeared to be just another regional traditionalist – was Raymond Erith, Quinlan Terry's mentor and partner. After Erith's death (in 1973) Terry carried on the practice. At first, he was tolerated – insofar as anyone took an interest in his work – as his late partner had been. Richmond Riverside marked him, in some people's eyes, as a dangerous subversive; but he soon had the support of the Prince of Wales for his efforts.

Leon Krier, whose work had been extensively published in Britain by *AD*, remained an influential theorist whose connection with practical building had ceased, it appeared, when he quit the office of James Stirling. But he was not content to be a theorist.

The Paternoster Square project, which forms the core of this issue, has brought together all key figures in the 'revival of architecture' (as Erith put it) in Britain. In addition, as a result of the way in which commercial development is funded, it has involved some of the leading American Classicists, heirs to a tradition with its own complex history.

Prince Charles lashed the proposals for the area by Arup Associates, Norman Foster, Richard Rogers, Arata Isozaki and others as mean-minded and arrogant: 'market forces', he declared, 'are not enough'. Leon Krier's criticism of the various competition schemes and his support for the unofficial rival drawn up by John Simpson was less about style than about content. It is hardly surprising therefore that Krier has not been a vocal supporter of the current proposals – for they do not provide for the mix of uses which he advocates.

Paternoster Square provides a considerable dilemma for supporters of traditional architecture. The proposed buildings are – apart from those by Terry, Simpson and Greenberg facing the Cathedral – essentially large modern blocks, dependent on artificial servicing and constructed on non-traditional lines. Yet the form of the scheme is, superficially at least, 'classical' and there is every prospect of a picturesque townscape which builds on the popular success of Richmond Riverside. What was never explored – and perhaps now never will be – was the application of a classically inspired masterplan in a pluralist way.

Paternoster Square could yet be a dead-end for Classicism. In any case, the very definitions of the 'classical' or 'traditional' urgently require rethinking. In Britain, Demetri Porphyrios has increasingly demonstrated his scorn for simplistic style-mongering and his recent projects at Belvedere Farm and Magdalen College, Oxford, underline his lively view of tradition and the positive force of convention. The Oxford scheme, in particular, shows him bending to the context in a way that the individualistic Quinlan Terry, interestingly, was not prepared to do when he added to Downing College, Cambridge. For Porphyrios, Magdalen is the embodiment of a living tradition which no architect should seek to pervert.

If Classicism in Britain has not entirely escaped from the old milieu of landed wealth and political conservatism, its connotations in the United States are very different. Thomas Beeby has been working towards a new civic style with his great library in Chicago – stylistically a blend of Chicago and New York motifs from the first decades of this century but at heart a big, rational building – and with his Rice Building at the Art Institute of Chicago. The latter is oddly but appealingly spare, almost stripped in style – like an internal version, one might suggest, of the public manner of Arup Associates in their Paternoster Square scheme.

The work of Beeby and Greenberg, Simpson and Adam, Terry and Porphyrios, exemplifies the central issue for classical architecture in Britain and America in the 1990s. How far can it continue to be an expression of a narrowly conceived view of tradition, a reworking of stylistic motifs necessarily applied to new building types? If Classicism is to make inroads into urban planning – and such is the ambition of Leon Krier – precedent is not enough. In this light, Paternoster Square, as presently conceived, is not the climax of a crusade but a stage in a continuing dialogue. *ACP/KP*

THE AGAS MAP, 1555

THE HISTORY OF ST PAUL'S CATHEDRAL
AND PATERNOSTER SQUARE

St Paul's Cathedral was founded in 604 and rebuilt by the Saxons in stone in the late seventh century. In 961 and again in 1087, St Paul's (and much of the City of London) was destroyed by fire and a large Romanesque stone Cathedral was gradually built in its place. In the early 12th century, as the Cathedral establishment grew, the Bishop of London, Richard de Belmeis, bought up lands surrounding the Cathedral. Further land was granted by Henry I and the ecclesiastical precinct around St Paul's was enclosed. This walled precinct around the medieval Cathedral is seen in a sketch map of London dating from the reign of Richard II (1377-99). Paternoster Row was a principal thoroughfare at the precinct's northern boundary, gated at St Paul's Alley and Canon Alley.

The Cathedral precinct at this time enclosed the Chapter House, the Cloister, the Bishop's Palace, the Chapter House or mortuary and Paul's Cross – the City's principal public meeting space. The Cross, an open-air pulpit from which proclamations and sermons were delivered, was rebuilt several times during its history before being demolished by the Long Parliament in 1643. Paternoster Row takes its name from the makers of Rosary beads or Paternosters who lived alongside the Cathedral precinct from the 13th century until the Reformation.

Other commercial activities in Paternoster Row, at this time, were all in some way connected with the Cathedral. They included stationers and text writers and by the early 16th century the area had become the centre of England's printing and publishing industries.

The Agas Map of 1555 shows the Paternoster site and the surrounding area densely packed with timber-built houses, on a medieval plan of streets and narrow lanes. Ivy Lane curves through the site from south to north where it connects with the Shambles and Newgate Market – the butchers' quarters and the meat market.

In the 16th and 17th centuries, Paternoster Row grew as a centre for silkmen and lacemakers. It was a way of life that was brought to an abrupt end when the City was razed by the Great Fire of 1666.

The Great Fire burned for five days and nights spreading through two thirds of the City. It crossed London in a burning arc from the Tower in the east to the Temple in the west and reached as far north as London Wall. On 7th September, 1666, Pepys wrote that he had seen, 'the miserable sight of St Paul's Church with all the roofs gone, and the body of the quire fallen'. Only part of Inigo Jones' west portico, erected during the restoration of

1627-42 and the Romanesque nave were left standing. After the Fire, Wren seized the opportunity to rebuild Cathedral for which he produced many designs including the New Model and Great Model Schemes, as well as the final Warrant Design of 1675. (Over the course of 35 years of building, the design was constantly modified and improved. The end result bore little resemblance to the early plans.) Within a week of the blaze, he had also submitted to the King a formal classical masterplan for rebuilding the City on a grand scale. Later plans prepared in 1710 by Nicholas Hawksmoor, Wren's assistant at St Paul's, show the Cathedral in a formalised setting, but neither scheme was realised. With thousands homeless and trade disrupted, the City had to be rebuilt quickly and this could best be done within existing property boundaries, using surviving foundations. The street pattern itself survived the Fire largely intact. Within ten years of the Fire, the reconstruction was complete.

Morgan's map of 1682 incorporates an early plan of the Cathedral and shows the reborn Paternoster area. It shows a widened Paternoster Row cutting diagonally across the site and a number of minor streets, such as Ivy Lane, intersecting it. The most significant change was the enclosure of the rebuilt Newgate Market within a new square. This replaced the sprawling *ad hoc* arrangement of street stalls that had existed before. By 1724, Wren had completed a modest brick Chapter House as a street building fronting St Paul's Church Yard.

Newgate Market re-opened after the fire in 1669 in a purpose built building erected within a new market square, thus establishing a formal relationship that continued unbroken until the area was destroyed during the Second World War. For almost 300 years, the street pattern in Paternoster remained virtually unchanged.

John Rocque's map of 1745 shows the incorporation of Wren's red brick Chapter House – completed four years after the Cathedral in 1714 – within a re-aligned St Paul's Churchyard. Indeed, comparisons of plans of the Paternoster site from Rocque's map to the Ordnance Survey map of 1873 reveal relatively few variations, although Newgate Street and Cheapside were widened in 1900. Any changes that did take place were in the style and height of buildings, and in the uses to which they were put.

For nearly 200 years, Newgate Market continued to operate as a 'white market' selling mutton, veal, pork and poultry but not beef. It closed in 1869 when the meat traders moved to a new location at Smithfield. In 1872,

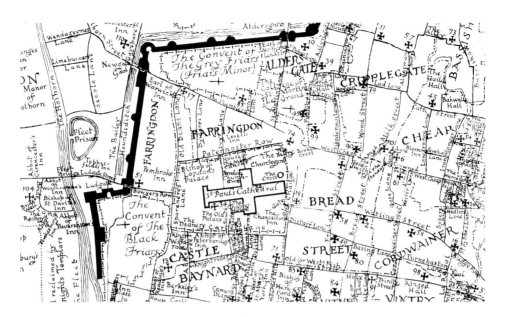

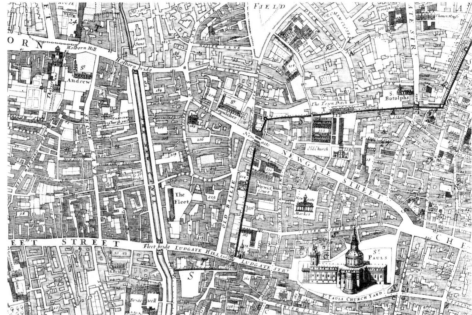

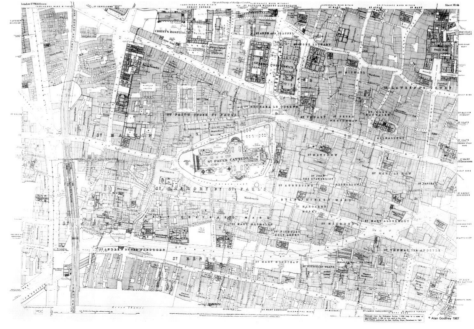

ABOVE: SKETCH MAP, 1377; *CENTRE*: MORGAN'S MAP, 1682; *BELOW*: ORDNANCE SURVEY MAP, 1873

the old market place was renamed Paternoster Square and the area was taken over by the printers and booksellers who already dominated Paternoster Row, a street that was to publishing what Harley Street is to medicine.

The Chapter Coffee House, which opened in 1715, in Paternoster Row became a natural meeting place for booksellers, writers and men of letters. In 1749, Dr Johnson founded the Ivy Lane Club at the King's Head Tavern in Ivy Lane and held weekly meetings there with his friends and literary associates. By the mid-19th century, the printing and selling of books provided the primary industry in Paternoster. In the second half of the century, other commercial activities were introduced to serve changing needs and tastes as the City evolved into the world's largest financial and commercial centre.

Between 1850 and 1900, many buildings on the site were replaced or enlarged, but still within the medieval pattern of streets and lanes. Among these were the textile warehouses and carpet manufacturing premises on Warwick Lane. St Paul's Churchyard was lined with a variety of commercial premises, shops and restaurants. In the northeast corner of the Churchyard, Nicholson's the drapers and next to it Henry Jones – a china and glass emporium – typified the kind of shops that catered to the genteel 'carriage trade' of wealthy City brokers and merchants.

The Chapter House too, responded to the commercial hustle and bustle of the Cathedral precinct. From the 1920s until it was gutted by fire in 1940, the ground floor was leased to Lloyd's Bank with the first floor serving the City Livery Club. Photographs of the Paternoster area taken around the turn of the century show a dense complex of streets and narrow passageways.

On the night of 29th December 1940, the dense urban grain that gave Paternoster its unique character was almost completely destroyed by a particularly heavy incendiary bomb attack. Intense fires spread unchecked among the tinder-like textile and print warehouses. It is estimated that over five million books were destroyed in Paternoster on that night alone. St Paul's Cathedral stood virtually unharmed while the world around it disappeared.

Just as the Great Fire had presented an ideal moment to prepare plans for the redevelopment of the City, widespread War damage was seen as an opportunity to replan the areas around St Paul's. In 1942, the Planning Committee of the Royal Academy, under the Chairmanship of Sir Edwin Lutyens, published a report on the replanning of London. Like Wren's plan, the Royal Academy's stiffly formalistic proposals were not implemented but had the effect of stimulating professional and public interest in how key sites in London could be planned.

In the 1950s, after more than a decade of debate and indecision, the architect and planner Lord Holford was commissioned by the City Corporation to advise on architectural policy, 'with regard to all buildings within the orbit of the dome of St Paul's.' Holford's March 1956 masterplan formed the basis for the present buildings which were constructed in the 1960s.

Holford's plan closely reflected the thinking of the time which rejected the traditional street pattern in favour of rigid matrices of building blocks and elevated access decks. Holford ruled out the possibility of reconstructing what had gone before. Instead, the few buildings on the site which had survived the wartime bombardment were bulldozed and the last traces of the medieval street pattern disappeared beneath a rigid planning grid set at right angles to the Cathedral.

Priority is given to vehicles at ground level, forcing the new central pedestrianised shopping precinct up to a raised level above service roads and car park. The buildings are horizontal slab blocks of varying heights. Holford's explanation was that, 'there is more to be gained by contrast in design . . . than from attempts at harmony of scale or character or spacing.' The Holford scheme was a product of its time, moving away from the traditional street pattern and compromising the historic relationship between St Paul's Cathedral and the City.

THE GREAT FIRE OF LONDON, 1666

ABOVE: PRE-WAR AERIAL VIEW; *CENTRE*: POST-WAR AERIAL VIEW SHOWING DAMAGE; *BELOW*: AERIAL VIEW OF LORD HOLFORD'S REDEVELOPMENT

THE URBAN FORM OF PATERNOSTER SQUARE

The city of London as it exists today is largely built upon a pattern of streets and lanes that has evolved since the Middle Ages. This has created an urban grain of irregular large, medium and small city blocks delineated by major traffic thoroughfares and enclosing pedestrian squares and courtyards fed by lanes and narrow alleyways.

The masterplan of Paternoster Square takes this pattern as its starting point for establishing an urban form. A network of streets, based on the traditional plan, including St Paul's Churchyard, Paternoster Row, Canon Alley and Ivy Lane will be reinstated. Paternoster Square will, once again, have at its heart a public square following a tradition established on the site by Newgate Market.

The Planning Application for Paternoster Square by Paternoster Association is for six main buildings for offices and shopping, arranged around a new public square with additional shopping below. This site is part of the masterplan, which has been designed with the flexibility to integrate the three corner sites at a later date.

The proposals for Paternoster Square present an opportunity to revitalise the area and unite St Paul's Cathedral with its surroundings. One of the main objectives of the masterplan is to construct buildings that are in harmony with the Cathedral and to restore views of St Paul's from

The Square whilst respecting the traditional alignment of St Paul's Churchyard and the Cathedral gardens, creating an enhanced public space.

An important aspect of the Paternoster approach is the re-establishment of the fabric of the City so that there is a return to a traditional street pattern and pedestrian routes. A new, traffic-free, public open space should be created allowing ease of access, especially for the disabled. The City tradition of classical architecture, using traditional materials such as stone, brick, tile, slate and copper will be recovered; although the architecture should be flexible enough for key corners, outside the Planning Application Site, to be integrated at a later date.

The Paternoster Association's emphasis on the pedestrian and architectural human-scale is a pinpointer to one of the masterplan's most outstanding principles, that is to breathe life back into the Square. This should be done by not only creating a thriving new business community in the best traditions of City life but also by providing a much-needed, new shopping area in the heart of the City, with a variety of shops, restaurants and entertainment, linked into St Paul's Underground Station. The new open public spaces should be enjoyed by office workers, visitors and shoppers alike.

WESTERN PROSPECT OF ST PAUL'S CATHEDRAL

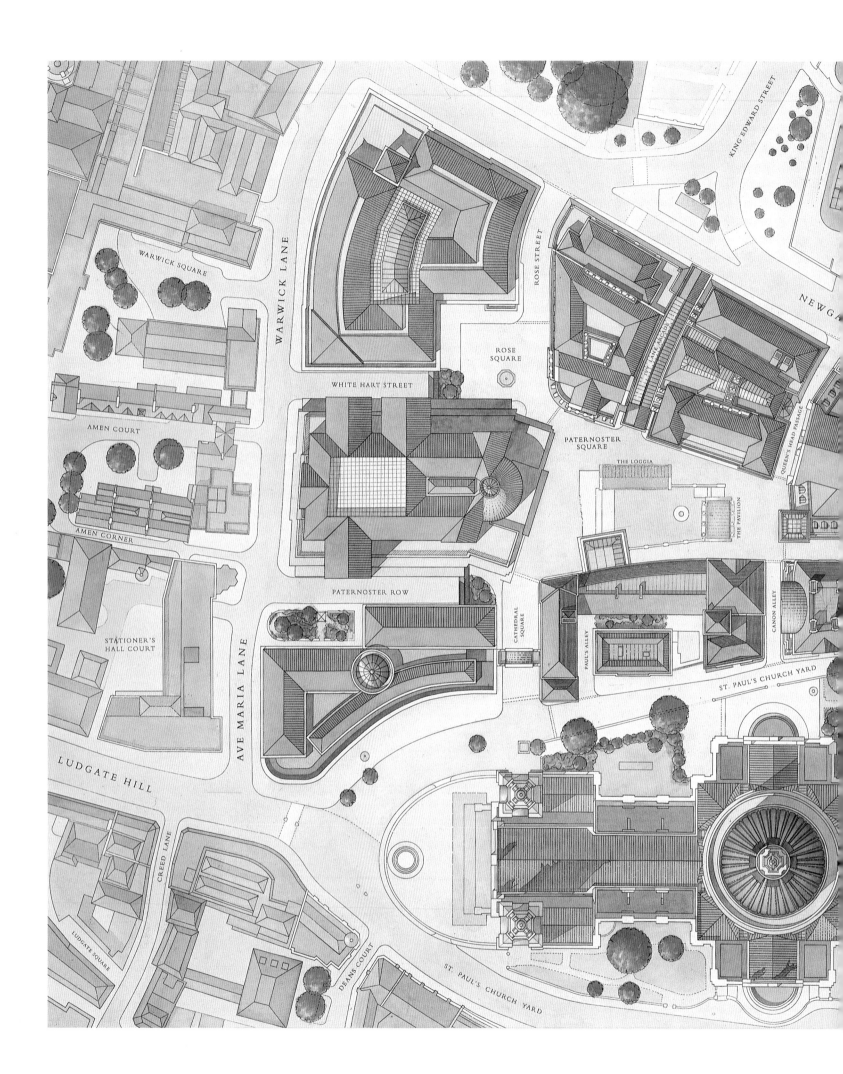

WARWICK SQUARE

WARWICK LANE

ROSE STREET

KING EDWARD STREET

NEWGA

ROSE
SQUARE

WHITE HART STREET

PATERNOSTER
SQUARE

AMEN COURT

QUEEN'S HEAD PASSAGE

WARWICK LANE ARCADE

THE LOGGIA

AMEN CORNER

THE PAVILION

PATERNOSTER ROW

CANON ALLEY

STATIONER'S
HALL COURT

CATHEDRAL
SQUARE

PAUL'S ALLEY

AVE MARIA LANE

ST. PAUL'S CHURCH YARD

LUDGATE HILL

CREED LANE

LUDGATE SQUARE

DEANS COURT

ST. PAUL'S CHURCH YARD

ST. MARTIN'S-LE-GRAND

CAREY LANE

FOSTER LANE

PANYER ALLEY

PATERNOSTER ROW

CHEAPSIDE

RAL GARDENS

NEW CHANGE

60

20

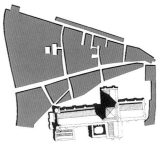

Hollar and Leake pre-fire map. This map, made before the great fire of 1666, clearly shows the medieval street plan, and a market on Newgate Street.

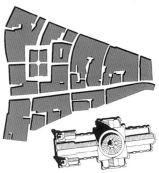

Rocque's map, 1745. After the fire the same street pattern was virtually re-established. Newgate Market moved into a purpose-built hall in a new square which, as this map of 1745 shows, provided a new focus for the area.

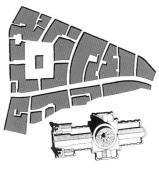

Ordnance survey map, 1873. Paternoster Row had been widened but there had been few other changes. In fact, the street pattern was preserved for almost 300 years – until the Blitz.

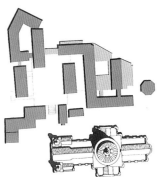

Holford's plan, 1956. This plan rejected the urban pattern of previous centuries in favour of a grid layout and raised access decks.

LEFT: Roof plan of the proposed masterplan

15

JOHN SIMPSON & PARTNERS, CUTAWAY PERSPECTIVE OF THE SQUARE

PATERNOSTER SQUARE AND ST PAUL'S CATHEDRAL

It is the masterplan's response to St Paul's, the City's greatest architectural and cultural landmark, which is a key to understanding the intentions of this scheme. The buildings facing St Paul's Cathedral will be aligned to restore the perimeter of the Churchyard. The railings lining the northern edge of the Churchyard will be returned to their traditional position, improving the pedestrian route between Ludgate Hill and Cheapside and enhancing the area of landscaped garden around the Cathedral. Four and five-storey buildings between Paternoster Row and St Paul's Churchyard will form sympathetic neighbours for the Chapter House and the Cathedral. The four-storey high cornice line of the Churchyard buildings will be continued as a unifying element around The Square, although the buildings to the north will be higher to mediate between the small scale of the Churchyard and the grander scale of Newgate Street. The curved streets and lanes of Paternoster Square will restore lost views of the Cathedral offering gradually unfolding views as St Paul's was traditionally appreciated. Apart from the processional route to the West Front, St Paul's was not intended to be viewed *en face*. From The Square itself, the Cathedral dome will command the skyline.

Paternoster Square will be established as one of the foremost shopping areas in central London. There will be more than 80 shops, including a quality food hall or department store. There are to be six distinct shopping areas: Paternoster Row, The Square, Lower Court, Ivy Lane Arcade, Newgate Street and the lower level shopping avenue. Paternoster Row has been reinstated as the main shopping street which links The Square with Cheapside,

the existing prime City shopping street. This will complement and build upon established City shopping patterns. The Square and Lower Court will form a focus for shopping and leisure with a mixture of catering, specialist and well-known shops appealing to City workers, local residents and visitors to the area. The Square will be linked to the Lower Court by staircases, escalators and lifts and will be connected to St Paul's Underground Station by the lower level shopping avenue lined with quality retailers and restaurants. In each area of the development strong emphasis has been placed on the variety of shops and services, from high-fashion women's wear to bookshops; chemists to gift shops; menswear shops to hairdressers. A variety of catering units will also be provided including restaurants, cafes, sandwich bars, wine bars and pubs. Many will have outdoor seating and will be open well into the evening. Emphasis will be placed upon attracting new retailers to the City.

A traditional approach to architecture will be continued at Paternoster Square since the strong precedents of classically designed buildings have served the City of London well since their development in the early 18th century. Leading architects have designed individual buildings within the masterplan of stone and brick to create a richness and diversity. The essence and real character of the City of London is captured by this view known in Edwardian times as 'The Heart of The Empire'. Here the unique combination of the medieval street plan and classical buildings, so typical of the City, is clearly evident. The ancient streets of Poultry, Cornhill, Lombard Street, Threadneedle Street and Princes Street converge.

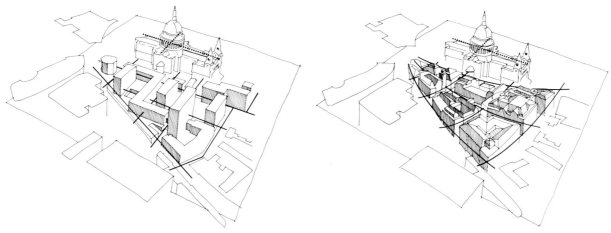

DIAGRAMS SHOWING DEVELOPMENT PATTERNS, *LEFT*: EXISTING SCHEME; *RIGHT*: MASTERPLAN

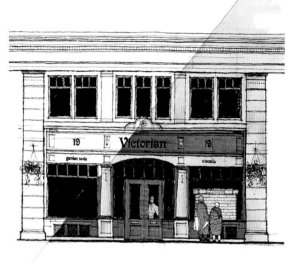

SKETCHES SHOWING PROPOSED SHOP FRONTS

18

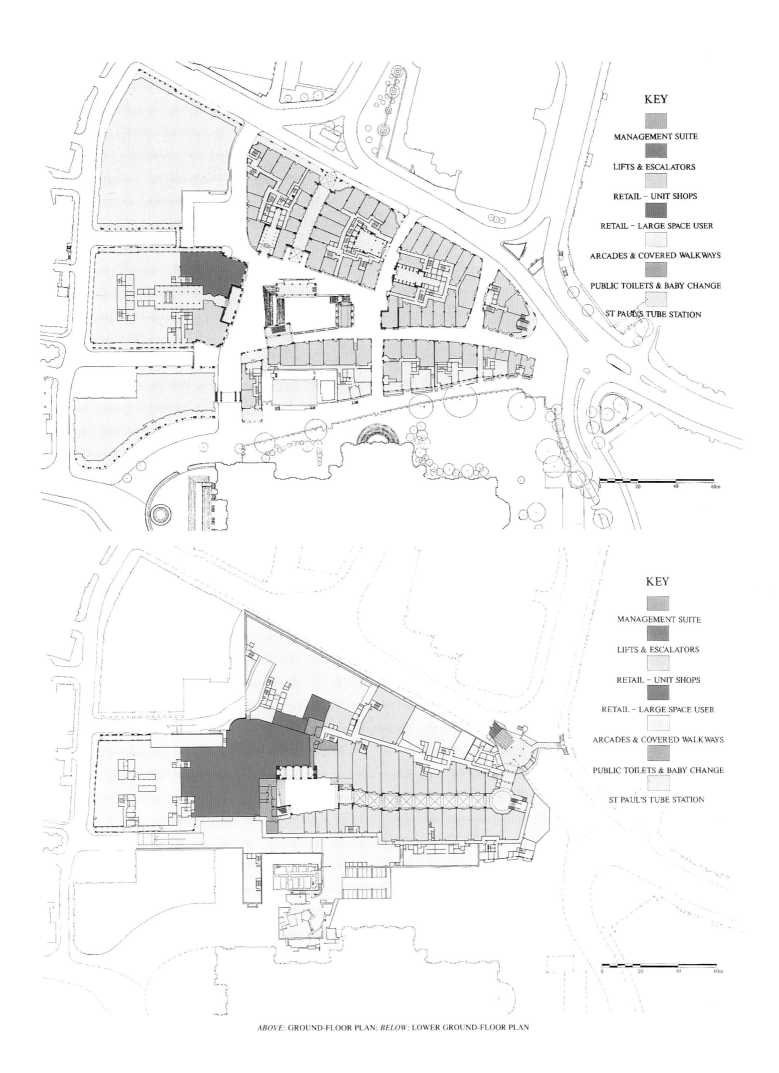

KEY

MANAGEMENT SUITE

LIFTS & ESCALATORS

RETAIL – UNIT SHOPS

RETAIL – LARGE SPACE USER

ARCADES & COVERED WALKWAYS

PUBLIC TOILETS & BABY CHANGE

ST PAUL'S TUBE STATION

20   40   60m

KEY

MANAGEMENT SUITE

LIFTS & ESCALATORS

RETAIL – UNIT SHOPS

RETAIL – LARGE SPACE USER

ARCADES & COVERED WALKWAYS

PUBLIC TOILETS & BABY CHANGE

ST PAUL'S TUBE STATION

0   20   40   60m

ABOVE: GROUND-FLOOR PLAN; *BELOW*: LOWER GROUND-FLOOR PLAN

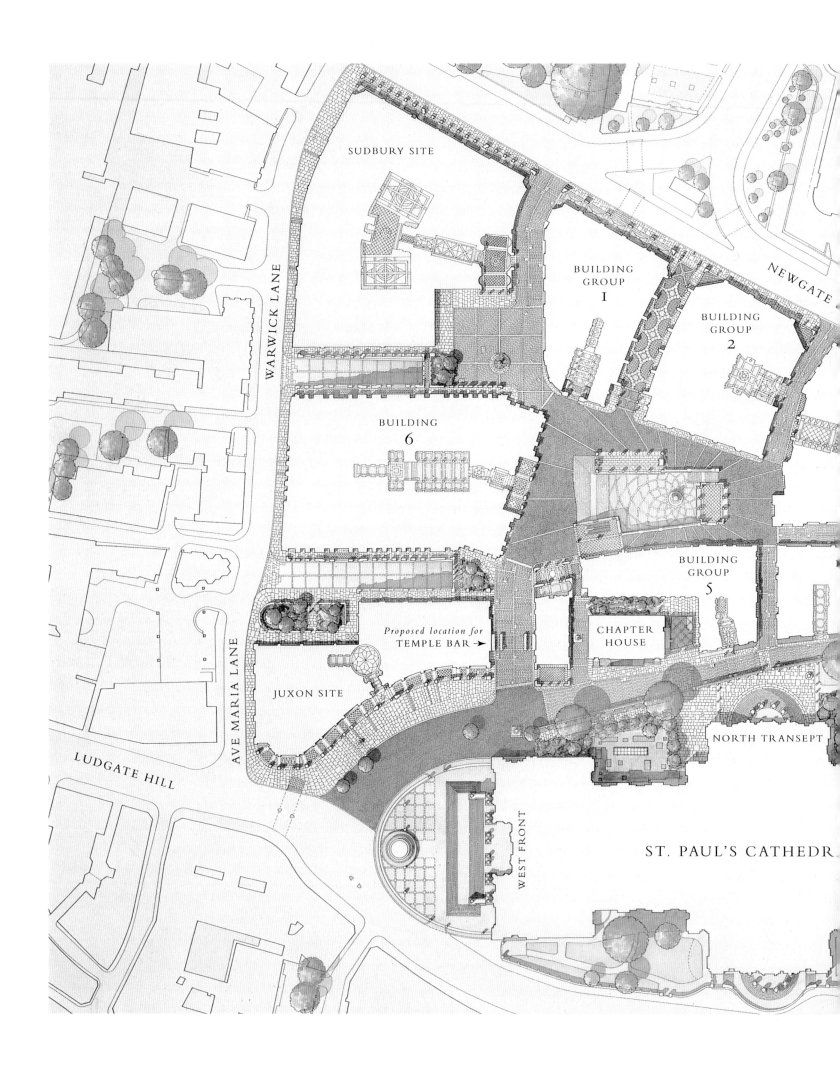

SUDBURY SITE

WARWICK LANE

NEWGATE

BUILDING
GROUP
1

BUILDING
GROUP
2

BUILDING
6

BUILDING
GROUP
5

Proposed location for
TEMPLE BAR →

CHAPTER
HOUSE

JUXON SITE

AVE MARIA LANE

NORTH TRANSEPT

LUDGATE HILL

WEST FRONT

ST. PAUL'S CATHEDR

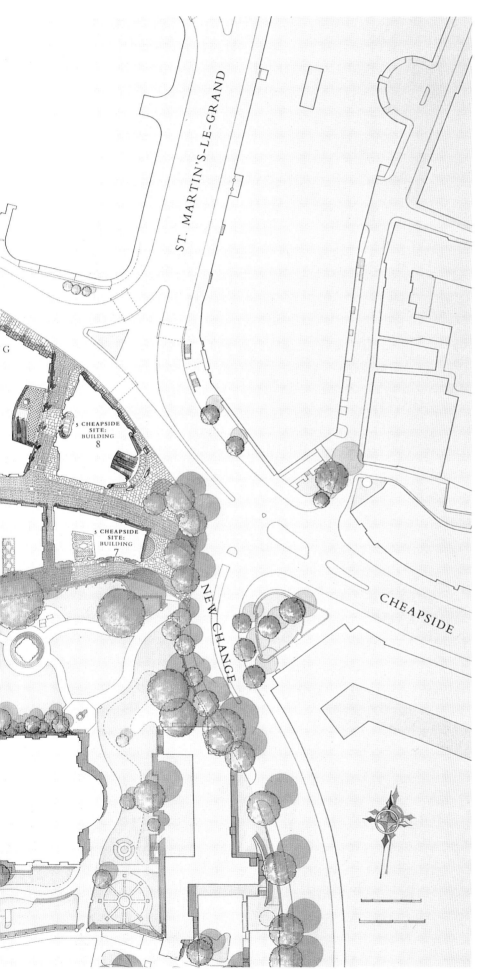

ST. MARTIN'S-LE-GRAND

G

5 CHEAPSIDE
SITE:
BUILDING
8

5 CHEAPSIDE
SITE:
BUILDING
7

NEW CHANGE

CHEAPSIDE

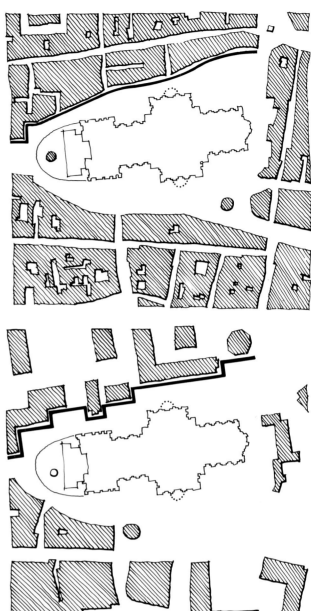

LEFT: The masterplan;
Diagrams showing St Paul's Churchyard: ABOVE: The traditional
alignment; BELOW: The existing scheme

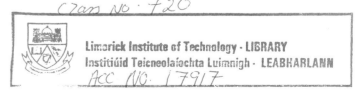
21

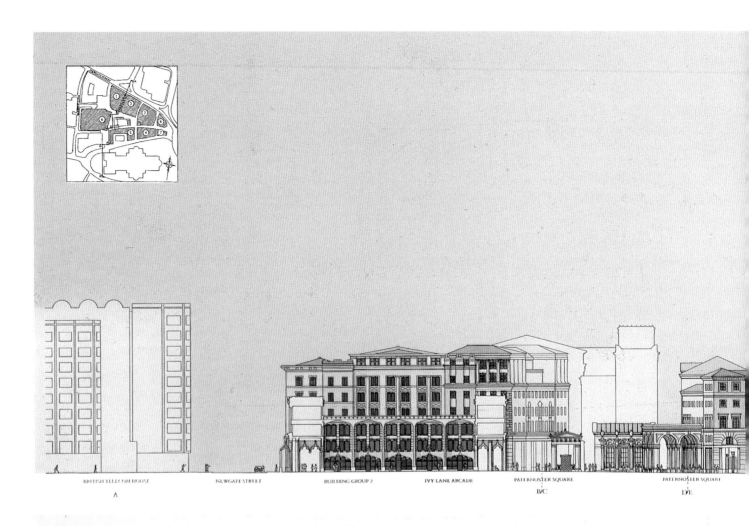

BRITISH TELECOM HOUSE   NEWGATE STREET   BUILDING GROUP 2   IVY LANE ARCADE   PATERNOSTER SQUARE   PATERNOSTER SQUARE

A   B/C   D/E

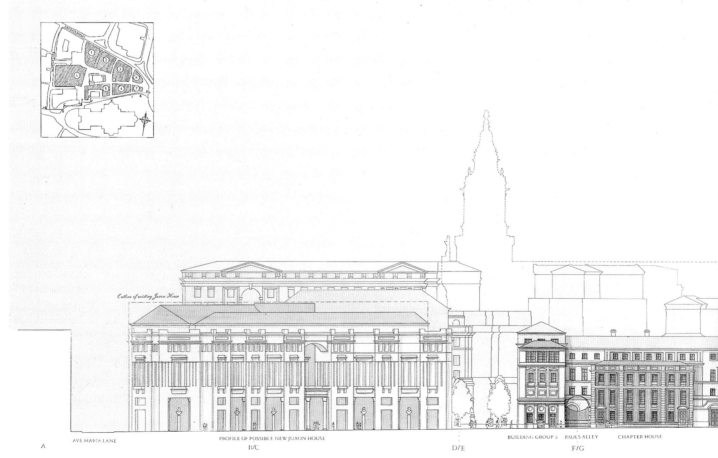

Outline of existing Juxon House

AVE MARIA LANE   PROFILE OF POSSIBLE NEW JUXON HOUSE   BUILDING GROUP 3   PAULS ALLEY   CHAPTER HOUSE

A   B/C   D/E   F/G

SECTIONS THROUGH PATERNOSTER SQUARE. *ABOVE*: VIE

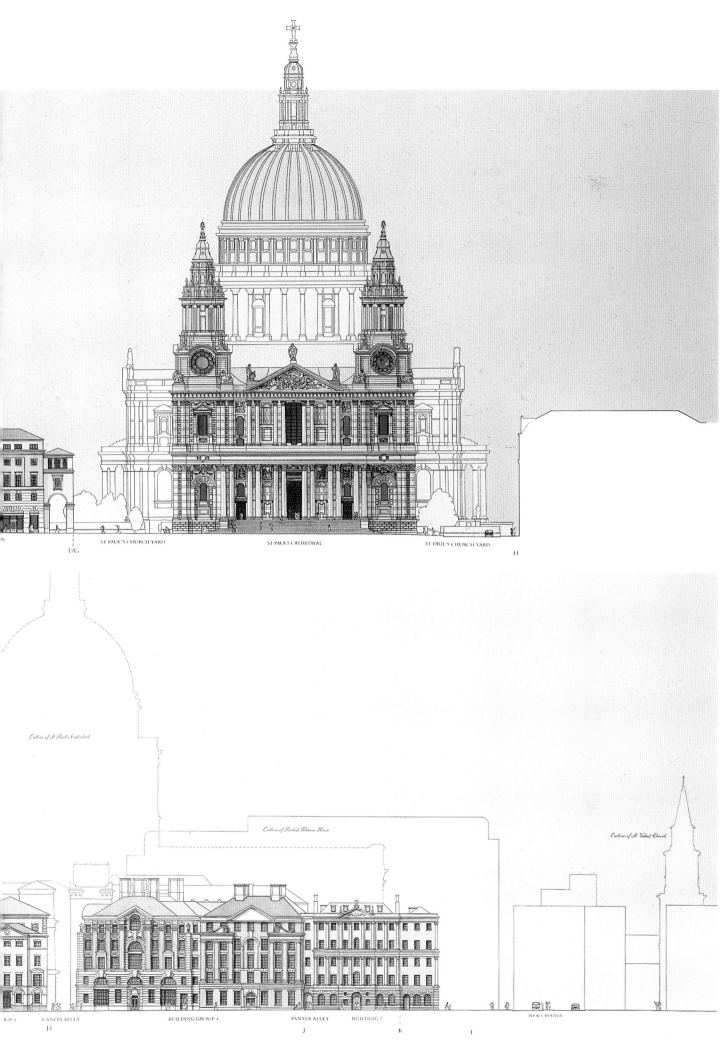

ST PAUL'S CHURCH YARD   ST PAULS CATHEDRAL   ST PAUL'S CHURCH YARD

F/G   H

Outline of St Paul's Cathedral

Outline of British Telecom House

Outline of St Vedast Church

UP 5   CANON ALLEY   BUILDING GROUP 4   PANYER ALLEY   BUILDING 7   NEW CHANGE

H   J   K   I

AST; *BELOW*: VIEW NORTH FROM ST PAUL'S CHURCHYARD

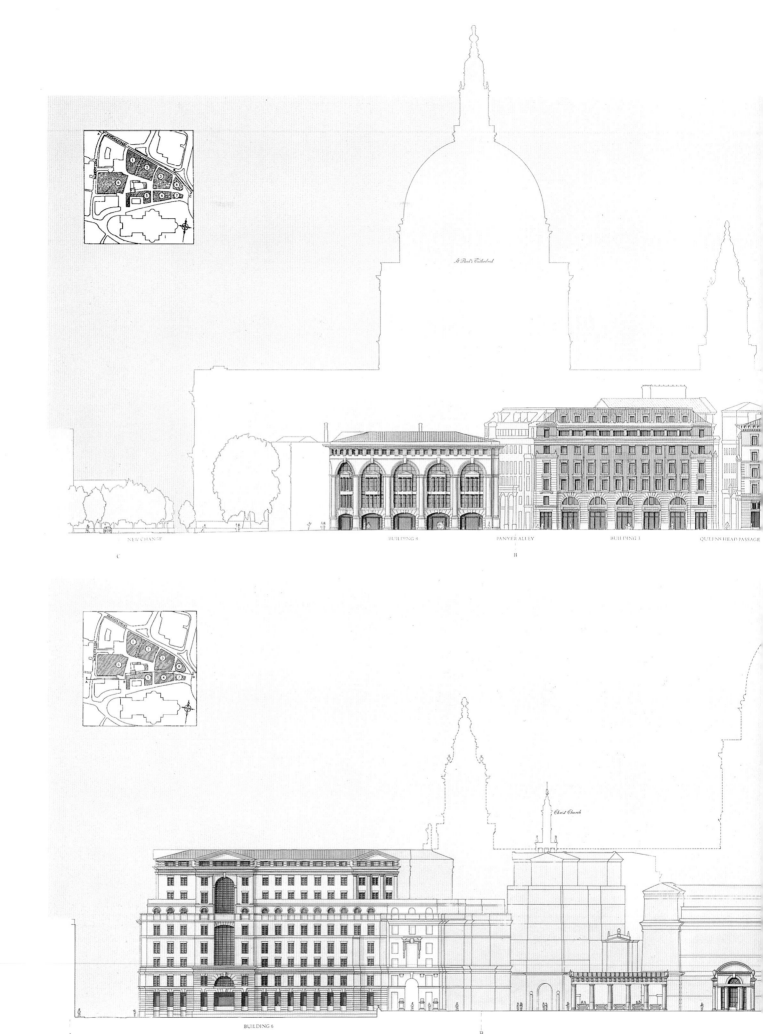

SECTIONS THROUGH PATERNOSTER SQUARE. *ABOVE*: VIEW SOUTH FRO

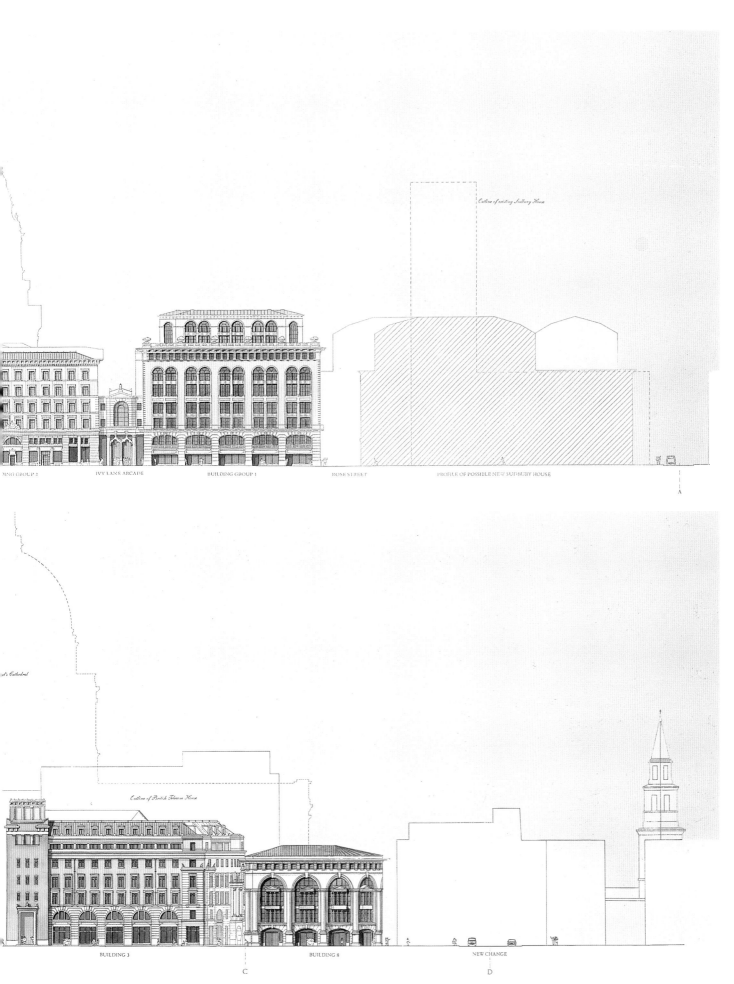

DING GROUP 2   IVY LANE ARCADE   BUILDING GROUP 1   ROSE STREET   PROFILE OF POSSIBLE NEW SUDBURY HOUSE

Outline of existing Sudbury House

A

Outline of British Telecom House

BUILDING 3   BUILDING 8   NEW CHANGE

C   D

EWGATE STREET; *BELOW*: VIEW NORTH FROM PATERNOSTER ROW

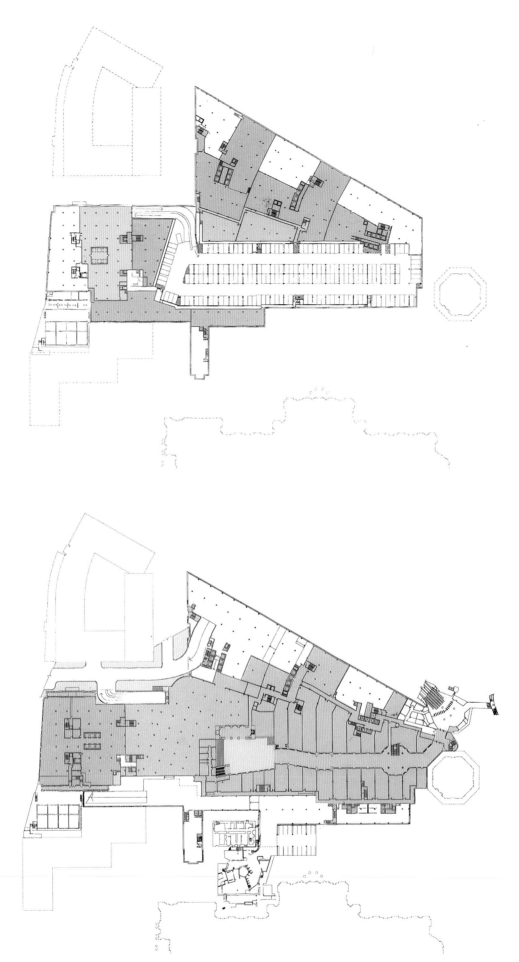

ABOVE: BASEMENT-LEVEL PLAN; *BELOW*: LOWER GROUND-LEVEL PLAN

THE PRINCIPAL PLANS

The following plans show the arrangement and extent of the planning application site, highlighting the intended variety of uses and their relationship to each other in the overall scheme.

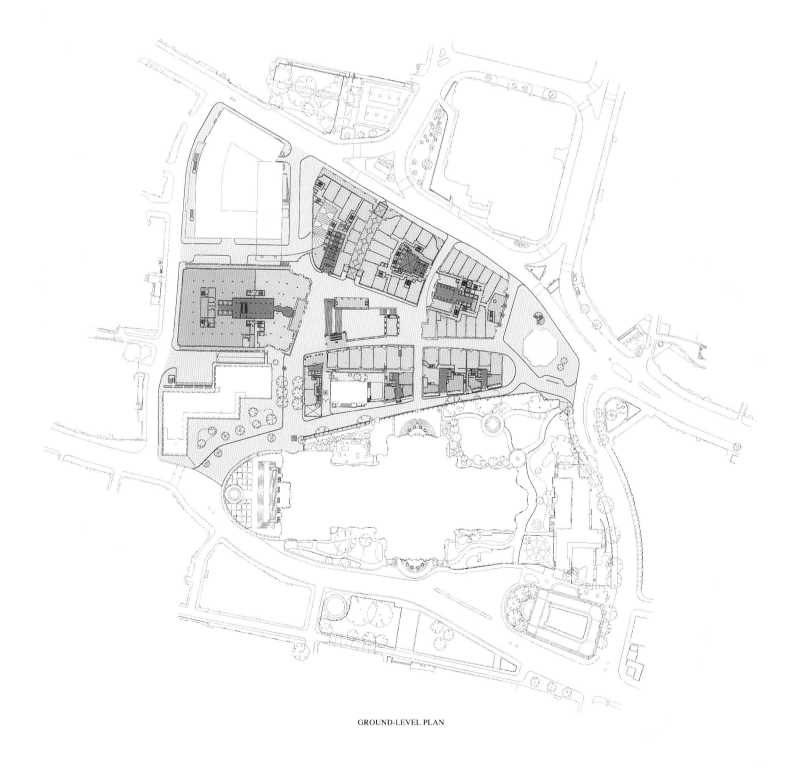

GROUND-LEVEL PLAN

ABOVE: TERRY FARRELL, PATERNOSTER SQUARE BUILDING; *BELOW*: SIDELL GIBSON PARTNERSHIP, NEWGATE STREET BUILDING

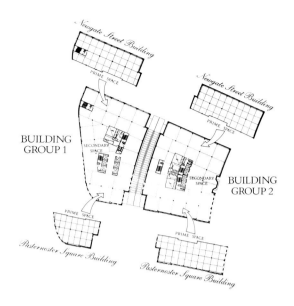

TERRY FARRELL AND SIDELL GIBSON PARTNERSHIP
BUILDING GROUP 1

Building Groups 1 and 2 are designed as a continuation of the urban grain of the City of London. Each has open aspects to the north (Newgate Street) and to the south (Paternoster Square), and restricted aspects to the east and west into the adjoining passage and Ivy Lane Arcade. These Building Groups are separated by the Ivy Lane Arcade which connects Newgate Street to The Square. The principal buildings in each group have been designed by different architects, working in collaboration and sympathy with the urban concept to respond to their particular context and views, as well as to the logic of the internal planning.

Terry Farrell, Paternoster Square Building
The relatively narrow frontage of this nine-storey building forms the northern boundary of Paternoster Square as viewed from the steps of St Paul's. The top consists of a tripartite portico capped by a pediment and set behind a balustrade. At
ground level, this centre-piece is echoed by a double-height entrance arch set within a two-storey stone base. The building continues above in brick with stone detailing. The top two storeys form an emphatic 'T' shape around the surrounding buildings. The centre portico is flanked by two further porticoes at right angles, which together address the Square and terminate views from adjacent streets.

Sidell Gibson Partnership, Newgate Street Building
This building looks onto Newgate Street and has been designed to reflect the atmosphere of commercial Clerkenwell and the workshops that have existed to the north of St Paul's for centuries. Classical proportions are used to add variety and interest to the nine floors by establishing a firm base, middle and top. At the seventh floor, the windows are incorporated into a Doric entablature, allowing the top two floors their own identity on the skyline.

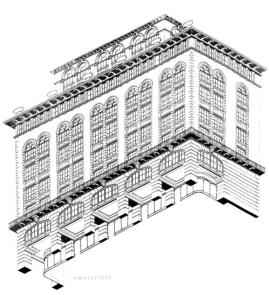

ABOVE: PRIMARY BUILDINGS; *BELOW*: SIDELL GIBSON PARTNERSHIP, NEWGATE STREET BUILDING, AXONOMETRIC

ABOVE: TERRY FARRELL, NEWGATE STREET BUILDING; *BELOW*: ROBERT ADAM, PATERNOSTER SQUARE BUILDING

TERRY FARRELL AND ROBERT ADAM
BUILDING GROUP 2

In its evolution from 18th-century practice, the Gothick shopping arcade parallels that century's development of Gothick as an acceptable variation, and development of classical architecture. This is different in spirit and content to the 19th-century Gothic revival architecture. Specific details have been taken for the arcade, for instance, from Batty Langley's Gothic Architecture Restored and Improved (1742).

A glazed fan vault roofs the central five bays, and classical pavilions carried on Tuscan columns mark the entrance from Paternoster Square and Newgate Street. Gothick detail unites the interior shopfronts with the entrances at ground floor. Above, two storeys of offices look in to the arcade.

Robert Adam, Paternoster Square Building
This seven-storey building forms a backdrop to The Square. Above a heavily rusticated Doric lower-two floors, the end bays have three floors in rusticated brick with stone details indicating an Ionic Order, which acts as a solid base for the

two projecting Corinthian temples above. Within the two-storey Corinthian columns are two lesser levels of small columns which emerge to form the walls of the top two floors as they step back to create roof-top terraces. The decoration is organised to represent the Church before St Paul.

Terry Farrell, Newgate Street Building
This building responds to the scale and the context of Newgate Street. It is based on a Renaissance palazzo, a prototype which provides a model for the window regularity required by an office building. There is a horizontal two-storeyed tripartite division. The stone base has set backs in the two end bays and is articulated with a major Ionic Order and subsidiary Doric Order. The ground floor is retail and the offices, which comprise the remainder of the building, begin on the first floor. The centre and upper divisions are of brick with progressively elaborated windows. The composition is completed with a substantial cornice at the upper level.

IVY LANE ARCADE INTERIOR, *ABOVE:* MODEL; *BELOW:* PERSPECTIVE

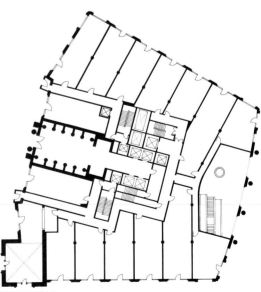

PERSPECTIVE VIEW FROM QUEEN'S HEAD PASSAGE AND GROUND-FLOOR PLAN

DEMETRI PORPHYRIOS ASSOCIATES
BUILDING GROUP 3

The emphasis in our design has been on the dialogue between architecture and the urban context. The geometry of the site suggested a building with many faces that is seen in fragments and never as a whole. Its massing, therefore, is designed to unfold as the observer moves through the surrounding streets.

There are two main entrances. The lower-level shopping avenue, with its link to St Paul's Underground Station, is entered from Panyer Alley while entry to the offices is from Queen's Head passage.

Along Queen's Head Passage the building is composed of multiple advancing and receding volumes which are ultimately centralised by the Doric portico and the crowning gable above. The tower marks the whole urban ensemble of Paternoster Square. It springs from the ground in a simple and unaffected manner and its unadorned surfaces contrast with the sculptural detailing of the crowning pavilion.

Vertically the building is organised into three sections: a rusticated base, middle and an attic floor. The ground and first floors are rusticated as are the corner pavilions. The terminating cornice lends the building a gravity and sculptural character while the gradual increase in the plasticity of the building from top

to base emphasises the accumulation of weight towards the ground. Ornamental profiles are used to underline the constructional reading of the building and ornamental motifs like anthemia, reeds, rondels and acroteria are used as punctuation devices or to soften the skyline.

The building has a concrete or steel frame with the external walls in self-supporting brick and ashlar construction. All architectural projections and rusticated surfaces are in Portland stone, all joinery work in hardwood and roofs are in copper or lead sheeting. Novel materials have been avoided for they have proven utterly unreliable in performance and have also resisted domestication. It is instructive that though 20th-century applied science and technology have made unprecedented strides, few of these have been of any real consequence to architecture. It is as if technology has forgotten architecture, perhaps in order to tell her that it has long ago reached maturity and perfection and that it should look for no further nourishment from it.

DESIGN TEAM: D Porphyrios, F Green, A Sagharchi, V Deupi
PRESENTATION: P Lorenzoni, D Anderson, I Sutherland, N Cox, J Papathanassiou, C Britton, M Kennedy, I Fleetwood

ABOVE: LOGGIA DETAIL; *BELOW*: DETAIL OF PATERNOSTER ROW ELEVATION

33

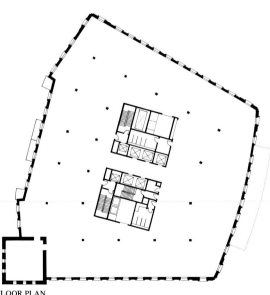

PERSPECTIVE VIEW FROM PANYER ALLEY AND TYPICAL FLOOR PLAN

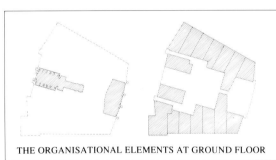

THE ORGANISATIONAL ELEMENTS AT GROUND FLOOR

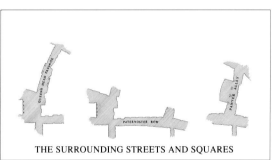

THE SURROUNDING STREETS AND SQUARES

ABOVE: QUEEN'S HEAD PASSAGE ELEVATION; *CENTRE*: DIAGRAMS INDICATING ORGANISATION OF THE SCHEME; *BELOW*: PANYER ELEVATION

TYPICAL SECTION WITH BAY ELEVATION AND PREPARATORY SKETCHES

PREPARATORY SKETCHES AND TYPICAL BAY OF LOGGIA

ST PAUL'S CHURCH YARD ELEVATION, DETAIL

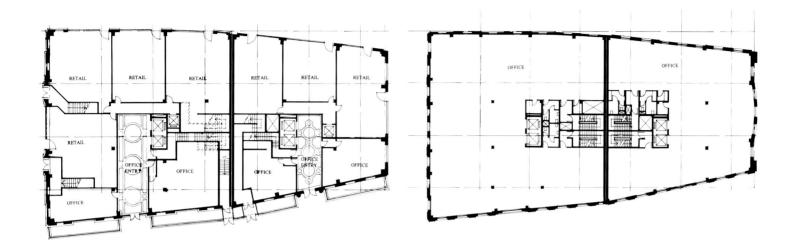

ALLAN GREENBERG
BUILDING GROUP 4

The design of Building Group 4 is a direct response to Wren's architecture at St Paul's and other places, as well as to the School of Wren from Hawksmoor to Shaw and Lutyens.

The architecture of Wren and his school is sculptural, rich in detail, and often dramatic in contrasts of scale. The keystones, round windows, ground-floor arcades, brickwork, limestone pilasters, metal railings, and other details of Building Group 4 are all developed from this body of work.

The two five-storey buildings in Group 4 are designed as totally independent structures, in conformity with the masterplan.

The two facades facing the Cathedral are inspired by Wren designs. The west building grows out of elevations proposed for this site by Hawksmoor: an arcade surmounted by a three-storey pilaster Order and attic storey. Further, the top floor

has much of its frontage set back with a terrace and balustrade. The east building has large windows based on the King's Gallery facade of Kensington Palace. Its taller, pedimented centre section was suggested by Richard Norman Shaw's Alliance Assurance Offices at 88 St James' Street.

Architectural attention on the Paternoster Row elevation is mainly focused on the lower two floors filling the field of vision for the pedestrian. The elevation on Canon Alley is simpler, focused on the two doors and shops. At Panyer Alley, the facade is gently curved to relate to the two adjacent buildings.

Materials are brick and stone. The bricks are of the same quality and colour as the Chapter House. The extent of stonework facing St Paul's Church Yard is limited to highlight the contrast with the stone Cathedral.

ABOVE: GROUND AND THIRD-FLOOR PLANS; *BELOW*: ELEVATION DETAIL

ABOVE: CANON ALLEY ELEVATION; *BELOW*: ST PAUL'S CHURCH YARD ELEVATION

ABOVE: PANYER ALLEY; *BELOW*: PATERNOSTER ROW ELEVATIONS

PATERNOSTER SQUARE ELEVATION, DETAIL

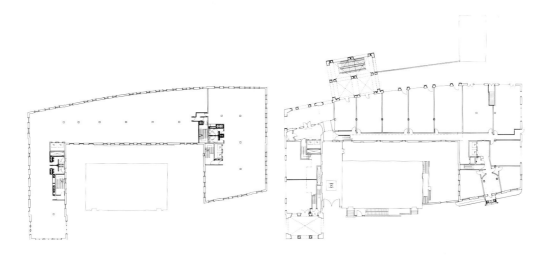

JOHN SIMPSON & PARTNERS
BUILDING GROUP 5

The new buildings in this group, together with the Chapter House, create an urban block immediately facing St Paul's Cathedral. The outline of the block follows the building lines of the pre-War street plan, redefining the edge of St Paul's Churchyard and restoring to the Chapter House the street setting for which it was originally built. Canon Alley is also recreated to the east of the block leading to the north transept of the Cathedral with the line of old Paternoster Row.

The height of the new buildings facing St Paul's remains modest – at four storeys – and below the cornice line of the first Order of the Cathedral. The size and width of frontage of each of the buildings is maintained in proportion to the Chapter House so that a street of buildings on a similar scale is created.

The buildings form the south side of the new Paternoster Square. Shops at ground level culminate at the west end of The Square, with a double-height, vaulted, open loggia which provides a way down to the Lower Court or The Square.

Within the block, Paul's Alley is re-created leading through an archway by the side of the Chapter House to the Churchyard. It provides a glimpse of St Paul's from Paternoster Square and re-establishes a sense of the scale and character that existed in Paternoster before the War.

The Chapter House Yard, at the heart of the block, provides an opportunity for a small private garden. Access to the Cathedral crypt and the Mason's yard are maintained below ground. To the west of the Chapter House is an open loggia.

As well as responding to their special context, these buildings have been designed to provide contemporary office accommodation. The block consists of two separate office buildings, one with an entrance off St Paul's Churchyard and the other off Paternoster Square. Each is then sub-divided into two further wings sharing services and a circulation core.

The buildings are designed to be modest and unpretentious so as to contrast with the Order and the architecture of the Cathedral. External walls are, therefore, predominantly in brick with stone for dressings and key elements.

ABOVE: TYPICAL AND GROUND-FLOOR PLANS; *BELOW*: ST PAUL'S CHURCHYARD

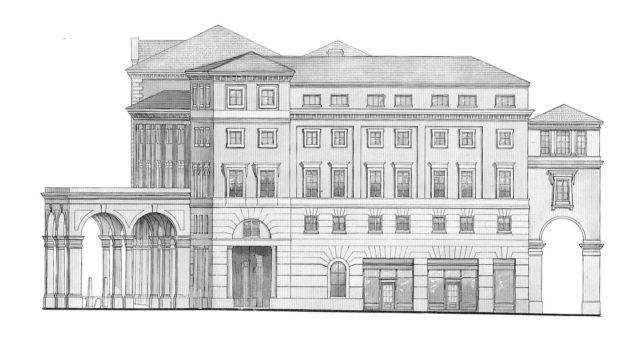

ABOVE: EAST ELEVATION FACING JUXON HOUSE; *BELOW*: NORTH ELEVATION FACING PATERNOSTER SQUARE

ABOVE: EAST ELEVATION FACING CANON ALLEY; *BELOW*: SOUTH ELEVATION FACING ST PAUL'S CHURCHYARD

PATERNOSTER SQUARE ELEVATION DETAIL, ATRIUM

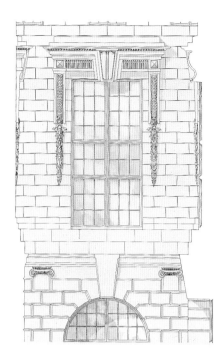

HAMMOND, BEEBY & BABKA
BUILDING GROUP 6

Our design approach was to synthesise the masterplan requirements for this block in a manner that would satisfy the demands of urban context, function and architectural character in the light of classical London office building traditions.

The masterplan guidelines set out the building footprint, number of floors and massing. The design of the building articulates a five-storey pavilion facing Paternoster Square, relating to the lower-scale buildings along the Churchyard. This pavilion shifts off the central axis of the normal building mass in order to visually terminate Paternoster Row, define the western end of The Square and provide a clear visual path into The Square from the west front of St Paul's.

Above the pavilion is a semi-circular feature which terminates the central mass of the building and provides a focus for a variety of visual axes around the site. The mass of the building is reduced and articulated along the north and south sides through a series of setbacks. These carry through to

Warwick Lane, creating setback corners and projecting bays which relate to the internal disposition of lifts and cores. The atria form the focal points for the semi-circular feature on Paternoster Square and the entrance lobby.

The need for variety in the urban context is achieved through variations in external mass, detail and materials. Facing Paternoster Square the materials are predominantly stone, and the degree of surface articulation is most overt. On Warwick Lane, an articulated surface of brick and stone enlarges to create a suitable street frontage.

This transformation at different levels on a unifying geometric and functionally derived framework is a method that responds to a variety of contextual concerns while maintaining the integrity of the building. The employment of traditional materials and a classical language that allows both individual and collective artistic contributions, represents a design approach that is deeply rooted in London's cultural heritage.

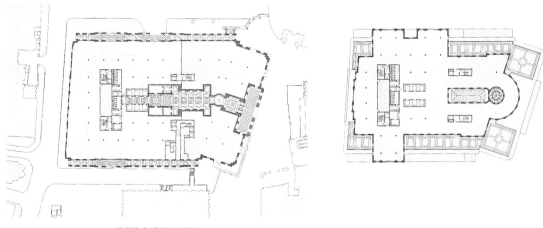

ABOVE: PATERNOSTER ROW ELEVATION DETAIL, PORTICO; *BELOW*: GROUND AND SIXTH-FLOOR PLANS

ABOVE: WHITE HART STREET ELEVATION; *BELOW*: LOGGIA DETAILS AND WARWICK LANE ELEVATION

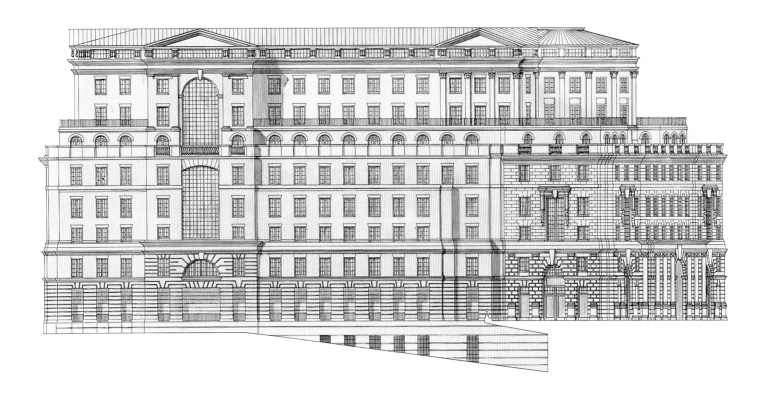

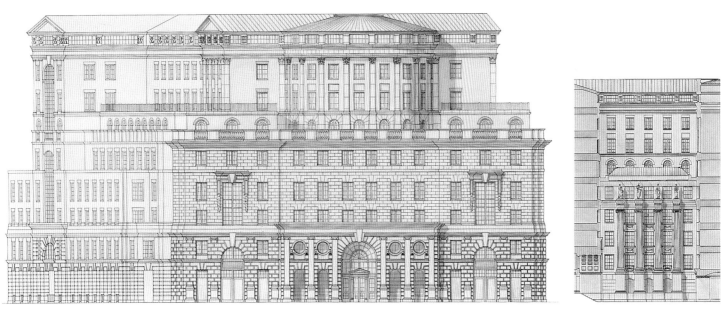

ABOVE: PATERNOSTER ROW ELEVATION; *BELOW*: PATERNOSTER SQUARE ELEVATION AND ATRIUM

PATERNOSTER SQUARE LOOKING NORTHEAST TO THE LOGGIA

HAMMOND, BEEBY & BABKA, DEMETRI PORPHYRIOS ASSOCIATES
JOHN SIMPSON & PARTNERS
THE SQUARE

The new Paternoster Square provides a variety of spaces with different characteristics and draws from the traditional English townscape of market squares, shopping streets, and arcades to support a range of public amenities.

The Square is at the heart of the new scheme. This new public, open space has been created as the focus of the restored street pattern and forms a natural part of the surrounding London townscape. Within The Square are three small buildings which together define a more intimate Lower Court. These buildings serve various functions, providing outdoor shelter and vertical circulation between the two levels of The Square.

The Loggia building to the north encloses a lift for the disabled and provides shelter whilst also marking the entrance to the large store from the Lower Court. A loggia attached to Building Group 5 encloses the Lower Court at its southwestern corner and houses the escalators leading down from The Square. The Pavilion is a two-storey building which overlooks the Lower Court and opens out onto The Square on both levels.

Two tiers of sweeping steps to the west of The Square lead from Building 6 to create a pleasant, informal, open air amphitheatre. The sheltered Lower Court is ideal for cafe and restaurant tables to spill into on sunny days, and has a large fountain at its centre with public seating. It also provides a link to St Paul's Underground Station through the shopping avenue.

ABOVE: THE PAVILION, WEST ELEVATION; *BELOW*: VIEW THROUGH LOGGIA AND VIEW FROM LOWER COURT TO THE PAVILION

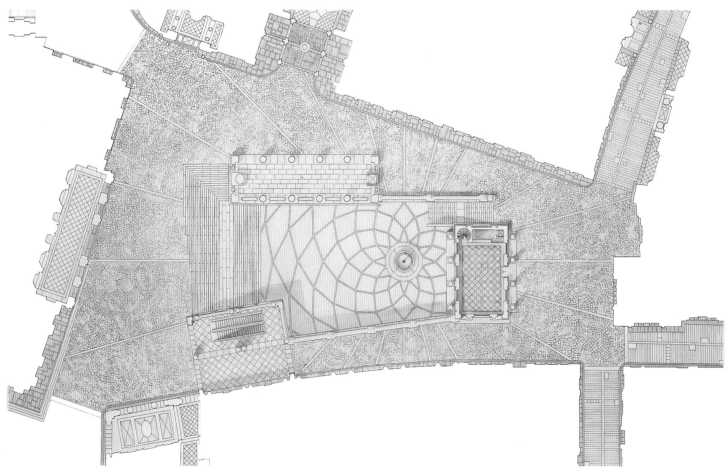

ABOVE: SECTION THROUGH THE SQUARE LOOKING SOUTH; *BELOW*: PLAN SHOWING LOWER COURT

ABOVE: AERIAL VIEW OF PROPOSED SQUARE; *BELOW*: PERSPECTIVE VIEW OF PROPOSED SQUARE

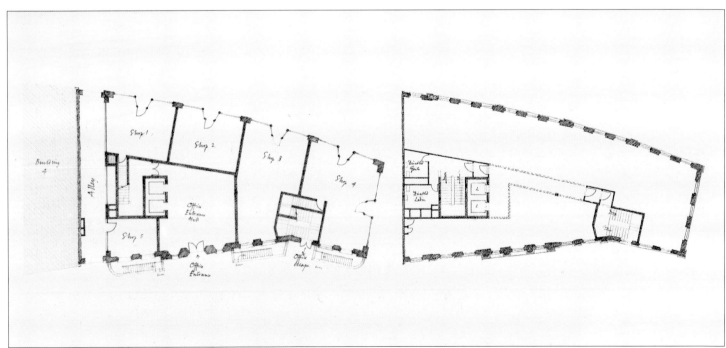

ABOVE: ST PAUL'S CHURCHYARD ELEVATION; *BELOW*: GROUND AND FIRST-FLOOR PLANS

QUINLAN TERRY
BUILDING GROUP 7

This is one of two buildings proposed for the 5 Cheapside Site and is a suggested design that shows one way in which the masterplan could be achieved. This building does not form part of the planning application by Paternoster Associates.

It was felt that this important site at the corner of St Paul's Churchyard and Paternoster Row should echo, in small scale, the architectural theme of the outer wall of the Cathedral which has a rusticated base and two superimposed giant Corinthian Orders. For this reason, the south elevation facing the Cathedral has a rusticated base which incorporates the office entrance and two giant superimposed Corinthian Orders, each with two floors of offices making a five-storey building. The general lines of the architecture continue at the east end and round the corner and back along Paternoster Row. However, the pilasters are more widely spaced to allow the wide span necessary for shops on the ground floor. Because of this, the east elevation is one bay with a wide span and pilasters at the corners, and the elevation along Paternoster Row repeats this theme over four shop fronts.

A photograph taken in about 1850 shows a late-Georgian building of this scale and proportion on the site. Another photograph taken before the War shows a five or six-storey ornate Victorian building on the same site. This design is similar in scale and detail to the earlier Georgian building. The architectural detail is traditional English Roman Classical employing the Corinthian and Composite Orders in the Palladian proportions complete with modillion cornices, pilasters, half-engaged columns and pediment. The rusticated base has many English and Italian precedents with its bold rustications of random courses with arches that are set over a fretted impost.

The building would be constructed in brick with stone rustications. The capitals and bases of columns, finials and other dressings would be in natural and reconstructed stone. The pilasters would be stucco on brick and the general walling would be London Stock with sash windows set in deep reveals with thin glazing bars. The parapet would be in brick with a stone capping, behind which would be a slated parapet roof.

ABOVE: NORTH ELEVATION FACING PATERNOSTER ROW; *BELOW*: EAST ELEVATION

WEST ELEVATION, DETAIL

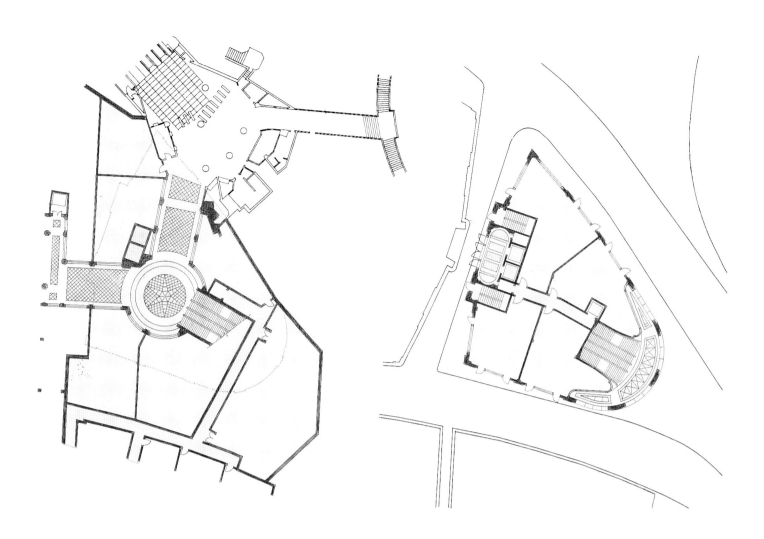

HAMMOND, BEEBY & BABKA
BUILDING GROUP 8

The second building proposed for the 5 Cheapside Site is a suggested design that shows one way in which the masterplan could be achieved. This building does not form part of the planning application by Paternoster Associates.

This building is in a key position at the natural head of Cheapside, when viewed from Poultry, and is on one of the highest points in the City. This site, with its long view into the City, is unlike any other at Paternoster Square and suggested a building that was monumental in character and yet modest enough in scale to comply with the St Paul's heights regulations.

The building's footprint is roughly triangular, its southern face looks out onto Paternoster Row as it curves in from Cheapside, and the apsidal east end continues to curve around to Newgate Street, maintaining the Continuity of the buildings on this street. The design approach was to create a building of monumental expression when viewed from Cheapside, but one that would reveal, at close proximity, a scale more in keeping with the detail of the

buildings on Paternoster Row.

The order of columns and arches that wrap around the building and contain smaller scaled window elements detailed in shallow relief reinforce the planar aspects of the wall. The larger Order creates a clearly defined object quality to the building that is further reinforced by an apsidal east end facing Cheapside and organised about a column on centre.

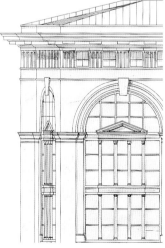

This eastern end also serves as a major entrance to St Paul's Underground Station and the lower level shopping avenue leading to Paternoster Square. The office entrance and service core is on the west side of the building, on Panyer Alley, providing the best outward views and maximum flexibility in office layout.

Traditional materials of brick and stone are used in the giant Order, with lighter metal and glass infills within each bay to achieve a smaller scale articulation at street level. Historically there are numerous classically inspired prototypes, developed in London through the centuries, for buildings of similar use on key corner sites.

ABOVE: LOWER GROUND-FLOOR AND GROUND-FLOOR PLANS; *BELOW*: SOUTH ELEVATION, DETAIL

ABOVE: CHEAPSIDE ELEVATION: *BELOW*: NEWGATE STREET ELEVATION

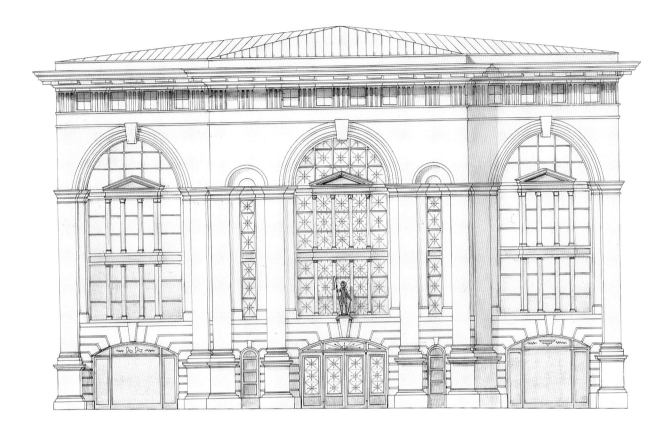

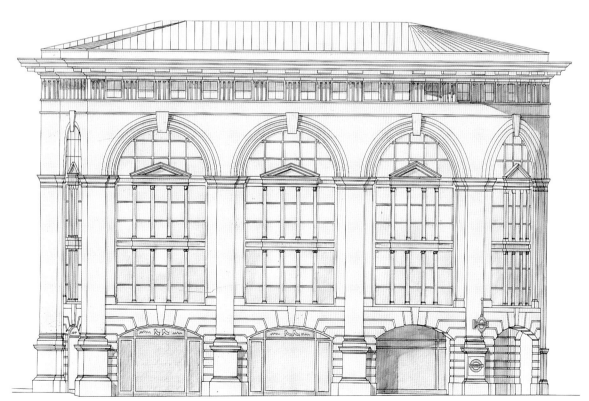

ABOVE: PANYER ALLEY ELEVATION; *BELOW*: PATERNOSTER ROW ELEVATION

ROBERT ADAM

THE LEGACY OF MODERNISM IN NEW CLASSICISM

The revival of classical architecture has been accompanied by a crusading fervour similar to that of the early Modern Movement. The relationship between the opposites goes further. The attitudes of many of the New Classicists themselves can be seen as a direct product of Modernism, the reverse side of the same coin, sharing an obsession with progress, technology and modernity. It is an obsession that could lead to the destruction of New Classicism.

New Classical architecture is only one aspect of the break up of the Modernist monopoly in the early 70s. Attempts to use history to liven up architecture such as Post-Modernism, Regionalism and the Neo-Vernacular generally did little more than add ill-digested bits of past buildings to essentially Modernist structures. Serious classical revivalists were only an isolated part of this great revolution and were at first dismissed as an irrelevant aberration.

Fierce conviction backed by genuine scholarship and a number of important commissions backed by public support have finally established a small body of New Classical architects as significant contributors to the development of contemporary architecture. The architectural establishment and architectural education, however, continue to be particularly hostile to Classicism. No classical buildings or architects receive awards from the professional institution and it is a brave student who tries to put classical designs in front of his tutors.

This combination of isolation and hostility, growth in the face of adversity, and the background of educational censorship have had a profound influence on the development of Classicism. Although most classical practitioners would like to deny it, the rise of New Classical architecture has been strongly influenced by the Modernist artistic heritage in which it has developed. In this respect late-20th-century Classicism is quite unlike any other period of classical architecture.

In antiquity and from the Renaissance until the 19th century, classical architecture was all there was. Even in the 19th century it was one of two dominant styles and it became the dominant style again in the first 40 years of this century. This is a formidable ancestry which encompasses its own history of change and development, revolution and reaction. Although late-20th-century Classicism draws on much of this history it can claim neither the dominance nor the universal professional literacy that accompanied the dominance of the past. As a

consequence, much of the theoretical background to New Classicism is based on a reaction to Modernism and herein lies its fundamental weakness.

The last 15 years of classical architecture have been a period of consolidation. From a base-point of zero, not seen since the 15th century, practitioners and theorists had to justify their existence in an atmosphere of professional ridicule which had never been seen before. The success of this consolidation was based on a growing public hostility to the excesses of the Modern Movement, and it is not surprising that the ideology of New Classicism should be based on a negative response to all that the Modern Movement represented.

In particular classical theorists have vigorously denied the two founding principles of Modernism: the theory of artistic advance through the avant-garde, and the supremacy of technological innovation. In Britain the process of re-learning has centred on the locally most popular and widespread form of Classicism – the Georgian – to the extent that all that is not Georgian is often described as impure or incorrect, and the term 'Georgian' in common speech is sometimes confused with 'classical'. The 19th century was further condemned in the eyes of New Classicists by the testimony of Modernist historians, led by Pevsner, who looked to the later industrial revolution for evidence of an immutable historical process which would lead to the enlightenment of the Modern Movement.

A negative stance to all aspects of Modernism is, however, in danger of throwing out the baby with the bathwater. In practice the denial of the importance of the avant-garde has, in the hands of more extreme traditionalists, become the denial of any desire to be modern; the denial of technological supremacy has become a sort of constructional fundamentalism where all forms of post-1820 structure and construction have been dismissed as un-classical; and the concentration on pre-1820 architecture has cut classical architecture off from its natural course of development so abruptly interrupted by post-war Modernism.

The quite reasonable idea that some avant-garde artists might produce work yet to be recognised by the public has, since the war, been exaggerated to the ridiculous idea that any form of popular appreciation of new art makes it automatically bad. This does not, however, mean that the desire to be modern, different and even shocking is unknown in the history of classical architecture. The idea that society is carried along by a sort of technological juggernaut driven by blind progress can be demonstrated to be incorrect. This does not alter the fact that classical architecture from the Roman arch onwards has adapted itself to new requirements. While it is hard not to admire the beauty of the various Georgian forms of Classicism, it is unrealistic to deny any validity to classical architecture produced in the 19th and early-20th centuries.

Although an appreciation of Georgian architecture cannot be a bad thing, the rejection of the concept of modernity (not rejected in the Georgian period itself) drives away much potential young talent. Constructional fundamentalism turns its back on genuinely useful technological developments and frightens off many of the commercial interests that lie behind many architectural commissions. If New Classical architecture does not look beyond a negative attitude to all things associated with the modern world – good or bad – it is defined to be a side show for ever and will fade into the oblivion predicted by its modernist detractors. As one of the small body of practising Classicists, this is a future I would like to avoid.

Where would a progressive attitude to classicism take us? Rather than engage in a fruitless attempt to predict the future, it would be more valuable to see where classical architecture had got to before its development was interrupted.

The 19th and early-20th centuries saw the introduction of not only new materials and manufacturing techniques but also more complex functional requirements. Classical architects did not reject these out of hand. Their deep understanding of classical architecture allowed them to adapt both technology and architecture to produce something both new and recognisably classical. Prefabricated cast-iron facades, such as Matear and Simon's Liverpool Cotton Exchange of 1906, were erected; steel-frame buildings were exploited for new design opportunities by architects such as Belcher and Joass in their 1908 Mappin and Webb building in Oxford Street; skyscrapers were not dismissed as un-classical but studied as a new compositional challenge giving rise to huge classical buildings such as the 30-storey Federal Court Building in New York City by Cass Gilbert Junior, completed in 1936.

If classical architecture is both to develop and expand it must re-establish this spirit of adventure. It must not use its enormously fertile past as a deadweight in a futile attempt to prevent progress but as a springboard into the excitement of the future.

SKETCH OF PROPOSAL FOR BUILDING GROUP 2

PAUL GIBSON
A JOURNEY TO PATERNOSTER

The collaboration with the seven other teams of architects designing the buildings at Paternoster has been one of the most enjoyable episodes in our practice's history. What was so stimulating was the combination of a broad agreement over the language to be used, enabling decisions to be taken readily, combined with strong differences of emphasis, providing different flavours and personalities for the separate parts of the scheme. As these differences obviously arise from the various routes we have all taken to reach our shared interest in Classicism, I thought it relevant to take stock of our own practice's voyage of discovery to this point.

Whilst studying in London in the late 60s two major projects jolted me into an awareness that all was not well with the way in which the city was being shaped. Leslie Martin was designing a huge office structure to replace most of the north side of Whitehall, including the Foreign Office. At the same time a GLC team was finalising plans to relieve traffic congestion in the Strand by running a six-lane sunken highway through the centre of Covent Garden. Both these schemes were not the product of greedy developers, but of serious designers with intellectual pedigrees. This was the era of Harold Wilson's 'White heat of the technological revolution', and no doubt the schemes would have 'expressed their time', but the results would have been catastrophic. There had to be a way of improving London that did not require so much destruction.

A little later, working for Farrell/Grimshaw Partnership and Foster Associates, I remember believing that any contemporary architecture that chose to use natural materials was just a joke. 'Folkweave' was the insult of the day. The fact that the buildings going up had dummy bolt heads welded on (Reliance Controls) or metal cladding fixed to obscure timber structures (Bean Hill) made no difference – the image justified the means. But a moment of truth arrived when, having set up our own practice, we were commissioned to design old people's housing in the centre of a Wiltshire village.

Was architecture that forcefully reminded one of its industrial production ever going to satisfy the aspirations of the old ladies who were our prospective residents? Clearly not. What they wanted were buildings that emotionally integrated them into the community, not separated them from it. With the initial thought 'if you can't do modern, let's do vernacular properly rather than some half-baked middle way', we carried out lengthy

studies of the more appealing older buildings and construction techniques of the area, before designing our housing at Pewsey. It was very striking to see how the older houses of the village, built of natural materials, had weathered beautifully, but the ten-year-old ones with modern detailing and synthetic materials already looked shabby.

These projects led to others in a similar vein, and the huge range of traditional British building materials gave us much scope to explore the variety possible within the format of simple terraced housing. It also became obvious that you don't have to look far in most villages to see that Classicism has become part of the vernacular. It was a short step to start using some of the details and proportions, for example the simple white windows contrasted with very richly coloured brown granite in Guernsey. When designing for the same client in a more urban context in Torquay, we chose to adopt the local stucco Classicism, and we were starting to experience just how effectively aesthetic and practical problems could be solved together if one did not reject mouldings and cornices. The realisation that we had evolved into 'classical' architects without deliberately setting out in that direction prompted more serious study of the subject, and consideration of how we might apply our knowledge to larger projects.

A recurring preoccupation with 20th-century architects has been the concept of honesty and truth as applied to structure. Yet the basic structures of large multi-storey buildings tend to be rather mundane affairs, be they of steel, concrete or masonry. This has led designers in different directions. One approach is to upgrade the structure itself to something more refined and highly finished, but this is an expensive process for a fire-protected tall building. Another option is to play down the structure and emphasise the elegance of the cladding, which can work if lightness and transparency are maintained. But a range of problems, from solar gain to partitioning requirements, make this approach difficult. Hence the cladding gets more solid. In engineering terms, the actual dimensional diminution required of the constructional elements as they rise through the building is so small that it is not visually effective, but the restraining hand of 'truth' forbids the architect to manipulate the design in a way that demonstrates that the building as a whole has structural stability, surely a basic human psychological requirement. Yet these are problems that are triumphantly solved in the best classical buildings. One could describe

St Paul's as a crude masonry structure totally transformed and elevated by the application of a symbolic and stylised system of construction, where the massive, simple structure is made expressive and eloquent by the imposed hierarchy of functionally exaggerated rustications and pilasters.

Our scheme for Grand Buildings in Trafalgar Square draws on these ideas, leading us to investigate a way in which the old facade could be improved by being given a more fitting sense of structure. The original building had suffered wartime damage and was missing many of its cornices. We could see that reinstatement of these would produce a facade of much more satisfying proportions, but the old buildings always had too little structure at street level – a common failing given the pressures to create large commercial shop windows. By incorporating a new arcade, the shops were free to express themselves without conflict with the facade, but more importantly it created the opportunity to achieve a really solid base structure for the building as a whole. Given these improvements, we thought it worthwhile to preserve the spirit of the original building, and try to reinforce the sense of identity and consistency in Trafalgar Square. The reconstruction approach to historic areas has usually had a bad press in the UK, though one suspects that the critics are happy to enjoy the 19th-century glories of Munich seemingly unaware that it was flattened in 1945, or to extol the architectural consistency of Paris whilst walking past its many replica buildings. Personally I rather regret that Richard Rogers' proposals to build the Inigo Jones designs for the Covent Garden Piazza were not chosen – it is a scheme that would have opened up the debate in a fascinating way.

Much of this debate has centred on the question of facadism, and this is of course a very real issue for the designers of office buildings for rental, where the interiors will change and evolve over many years. There have been projects which seek the dramatic contrast of Modernism in a historical setting, Foster Associates' new galleries at the Royal Academy being one of the most brilliantly successful. At Grand Buildings we worked with a different strategy, which was to seek out and emphasise those elements that would provide continuity. At the moment the facade is probably taken by most to be the original 19th-century one cleaned up. I say 'at the moment' deliberately because it is not actually a replica, and I believe that in retrospect all design work is eventually perceived, and datable, as an expression of its own times. The entrance halls using stone in continuity with the facade lead to an atrium which has imagery derived from the 19th-century winter garden, but is essentially an expression of a 20th-century structure using classical proportions. This leads to the office floors

themselves, which still use vestigial Classicism in the form of flat cornices around the demountable ceilings and window surrounds with keystones.

Other current projects draw on Classicism rather than use it explicitly. At Hay Hill in Mayfair we have accepted an expression of a simple framed structure, but clad it with stone and used cornices and capital-like junction pieces to increase the richness and modelling. Another project, in central Frankfurt, uses a similar language but this time with metal cladding. Modern offices are rightly designed to cater for change and adaptability, which results in extremely standardised floor heights and window modules. But how often has this led to the interminable wallpaper facades that have ruined so many cities. The lesson that we are trying to learn from the classical tradition is the way in which a hierarchy of constructional elements can be overlaid on this standardisation to give an obvious comprehensibility to the whole.

Our building at Paternoster looks away from the main square, and we have seen it not so much as part of the Cathedral precinct, but as relating to the traditional areas for workshops and small businesses to the north. Walking around Clerkenwell one is struck by the many noble buildings in the warehouse tradition which gain their effect not by expressing complex social distinctions, or by displaying elaborate ornamentation, but by the elegance of their constructional elements. These buildings were our starting point. We have taken the main structure frame and dramatised it with four-storey-high openings, topped with an entablature that is consequently at a size that can accommodate a whole floor. We have been able to introduce an arcade at ground level, which allows us to provide the required substantial base. Into the larger openings are inserted two-storey-high window elements defined by the rusticated brick pilasters at their sides. The window units themselves act structurally, supporting the masonry above on their own system of cast metal columns. Thus the facade is thought of in three superimposed layers progressing down from an implied giant order, in scale with the boulevard that Newgate Street is to become, down to the human scale of individual windows.

Our fascination with Classicism is directed towards the mechanics of construction made visible in a refined way, and we see no reason why the language should be held to be the expression of a defunct social order. We would relish on occasion the opportunity to try to develop the language with new materials and techniques. At the same time, we respect the deep need of most citizens to feel that their cities are places of quiet continuity, and for this reason we are delighted to be able to participate at Paternoster Square in a scheme that so ambitiously tries to re-establish a continuity that is conspicuously missing there today.

ALLAN GREENBERG
MAKING ARCHITECTURAL JUDGEMENTS

SECTIONS
OF
CLASSICAL MOULDINGS

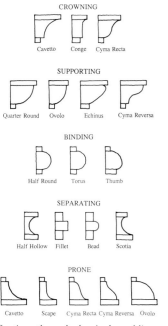

CROWNING

Cavetto — Conge — Cyma Recta

SUPPORTING

Quarter Round — Ovolo — Echinus — Cyma Reversa

BINDING

Half Round — Torus — Thumb

SEPARATING

Half Hollow — Fillet — Bead — Scotia

PRONE

Cavetto — Scape — Cyma Recta — Cyma Reversa — Ovolo

Sections through classical mouldings. Adapted from Study of the Orders *by Frank Chouteau Brown, Frank A Bourne, and Herman V Von Holst, Chicago, 1921.*

How should an architect, a client, a citizen, or a government agency or commission judge designs for new buildings?[1] This question is especially pertinent if the new structures are to be erected in historic districts. How does one decide whether the proposed new building will enhance or detract from its surroundings, and whether it will promote the kind of further development that will benefit the historic area? What criteria can be used as a basis for such judgements? Do the answers lie in adhering to some 'correct' architectural ideology derived from a classical, a modernist, or a post-modernist point of view to be handed down by 'experts'? Does the task require studied connoisseurship, group consensus growing out of broad public participation, or some combination of these positions?

The need for a more rational approach to these questions is evident from the nature of the discussion that has surrounded recent controversial buildings, in which reasonable differences of opinion have often devolved into vituperative confrontations. The differences among opposing groups often hinge on passionately held beliefs about aesthetics, politics, or such vague notions as the demands of the *Zeitgeist*, the 'spirit of the times'. The focus on subjective questions of taste, ideology, and personality tends to discourage constructive debate and to ignore more complex and pertinent questions of how to protect the public interest.

The depth of this problem may be seen by reviewing the weak and conflicting statements of problems that are presented within transcripts of hearings before boards and commissions with purview over architectural projects, and by reading their subsequent reports. Anyone who has attended juries evaluating students' work at schools of architecture will be familiar with the subjective criteria that often pass for considered, objective judgements. Because decision-making bodies cannot evade their responsibilities, this haphazard, emotion-laden way of defining architectural standards has created the incoherently planned cityscape, the suburban sprawl, and the suburbanised countryside we see around us.

This contemporary dilemma should be considered in its proper historical context. The generations of architects since 1945 are the first in the history of architecture who have not been able to fulfil two expectations that society has taken for granted since the ancient Greeks created cities: that architects are able to create both the competently designed background architecture that forms the bulk of building in a town or city, as well as noble foreground buildings, the monumental architecture of civic and religious structures that embodies a society's highest aspirations. It was in this way that architects of the past arranged their designs in city plans so as to make the new as beautiful, or better than, what was there before. Remarkable examples of this abound: Jacopo Sansovino's inspired 're-creation' of the Piazza di San Marco and the Piazzetta, accomplished by transforming the Campanile into a free-standing tower and fulcrum to connect Piazza with the Piazzetta, and the brilliant design of the new Library and Zecca; JF Blondel's classical facade of the medieval Metz Cathedral (1764),[2] sadly destroyed, and new adjacent buildings; Mnesicles' Propylaea at the Acropolis; and Wren's buildings at Oxford and Cambridge. To revitalise contemporary practice to meet the standards of the past is an urgent responsibility.

Architecture is a liberal art that is taught at our great universities, and is a discipline that should be amenable to rational discourse. The aim here is not to decide on the ultimate artistic worth of a proposed building, for this requires the kind of considered assessment that, ultimately, only the distance of time can provide. Instead, it is to suggest a process that may assist us in evaluating the quality of proposed designs for new architecture in a variety of historic areas, a way of deciding whether the proposal at hand will add to or detract from the beauty and character of the place. The process offers a set of criteria which can help to make distinctions between the architectural characteristics of a proposed building and to relate them to those of the buildings which exist around its site. Once articulated, these distinctions provide a common basis for concerned citizens, critics, decision-making bodies and architects to debate the drawbacks and virtues of the design and to prepare a solid foundation for a decision to accept or to improve or otherwise modify the design or programme.

Architecture is a public art. It is the building block of the city, a compound work, realised over centuries. Cities are always changing, growing and being altered, being destroyed and being rebuilt, all in response to social and political change, to the demands of commerce and industry, and to the rhythms of technological innovation. Villages and rural areas are subject to the same pressures.

Each time a new building is proposed it must be studied, not in isolation, but evaluated as a part of the increasingly complex whole that forms all cities and regions.

Evaluating Proposed Architecture in Historic Areas
Perhaps the best place to begin to develop criteria for evaluating new designs for historic areas is with a working definition of architecture. The one that follows is a synthesis of the ideas of Geoffrey Scott and Le Corbusier, as well as those gleaned from my own practice: 'Architecture, simply and immediately perceived, is a combination, revealed through light and shade, of spaces, of masses, and of lines,'[3] which embody the meaning and significance of the institution housed within its walls. It should enhance its environs and serve as a paradigm for future development.

The definition suggests five criteria which may be used for guidance in assessing the relationship between a proposed new design and its context. The first is architectural language, which has two components: forms and grammar. Forms are the orders of architecture: the columns and entablatures of the Doric, Ionic, Corinthian, composite, and Tuscan orders, and the mouldings. The latter are a set of specific forms which have a precisely determined geometric shape and a name. Grammar is the set of conventions by which these elements are arranged to form coherent elements, or parts, of buildings. These may be conventional and compound architectural forms such as cornices, pediments, architraves, serliana, dadoes, baseboards and plinths. Grammar also determines specific conventions governing the use of planning devices such as grids and axes. The classical language of architecture contains the most highly developed grammar, which uses forms to create plans, sections, and elevations of buildings, rooms, streets (which may be considered as walls of exterior rooms) and groups of buildings. Gothic, Byzantine, and Romanesque architecture use many of the elements and aspects of the grammar of classical architecture. Like the less complex and elaborate architectural language of Japan or of the Maya, classical architecture is tied to a particular time, place, culture and geography. Thus the architectural language of the 17th century in Venice is different from that of France or of England, although all three are classical and contemporary. Modernistic architecture has its own forms – *piloti*, horizontal window bands – and grammar. Both are derived from the work of Le Corbusier, Mies van der Rohe, Auguste Perret and Walter Gropius, and they are newer and therefore much less developed than classical or Gothic architecture.

The second criterion, architectural syntax, consists of organising systems that are fundamental to the perception of architectural form and space. These include rhythm, sequence of spaces, differentiation of scale, notions of order, reflection, translation, superimposition, the tension between interior and exterior, the relationship of solid and void or of mass and volume, inflection, and

ideas of unity. All are properties of form, and they transcend the particularities of style and culture.

The third criterion, that of context, which may be urban, suburban, village or rural, posits the character of the relationship between the new building and the neighbourhood. This should be analysed in terms of formal characteristics and of relationships to physical infrastructure of public works, as well as of questions which transcend architectural form and encompass relevant law and ordinances, as well as custom and tradition (mores).

In exploring these concerns, it is sometimes easy to slough off custom and tradition as a mere collection of arbitrary value judgements. Yet it is precisely these elements that are often crucial to the success of any project.[4] The history of the many failures of subsidised housing projects in England and the United States illustrates the folly of ignoring the most basic consideration of our human need for dignity and respect, as well as how easily noble intentions can blight communities and create human misery.

The fourth criterion is symbolic content, the articulation of meaning and significance projected by architectural forms through their language, syntax, and relation to their context.[5] Like customs and traditions, it has been ignored for the past 50 years by architects. For example, the beautiful door of the Hammond-Harwood House (1770-74) in Annapolis is framed by an arch set within attached columns and a pediment. It is a unique feature of the facade and clearly marks the entrance. Its large scale within the facade diminishes the building's scale in order to mediate between the size of the building and a human being. The symmetrical and obvious location of the beautiful door, as well as its superb scale and proportion, makes a gracious gesture of welcome.

These meanings grow out of anthropomorphism and traditional and conventional usage. We associate the pediment and supporting columns of the Hammond-Harwood house door with the temples of ancient Greece and Rome, where the pediment form was associated with the gods, and the column was interchangeable with the human form. Its use in 18th-century American domestic architecture tells us that the rights and prerogatives which were once the prerogatives of the gods of the ancient world, and the monarchs of Europe, belong, in the New World, to all citizens. The human form of the two attached columns supporting the pediment allows the viewer to imagine being at home in the house. The symbolic content of these design decisions is what relates architecture to the life of a community and culture. It is the architect's job to realise this life by reflecting it in the nature of the design.

Symbolic content depends upon the subtle articulation of both architectural language and architectural syntax. If the classical columns and pediment were removed, the anthropomorphism would be lost, as would the symbolic content. We would be left with a building and an opening

William Buckland, Hammond-Harwood House, Annapolis, Maryland, street facade.

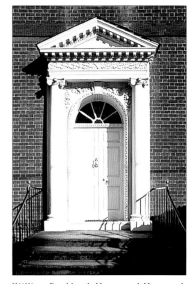

William Buckland, Hammond-Harwood House, Annapolis, Maryland, detail of the entrance door.

R Clipson Sturgis, house in Seaview Terrace, Bridgeport, Connecticut. The architect and client (the US government) provided housing for the poor which is similar in character and thoughtful planning to homes of the wealthier classes.

S P Fuller, Louisburg Square, Boston, laid out in 1826. The houses around the square were built between 1834 and 1848.

with a door. For example, if the size of the door were increased or decreased relative to the size of the building, the scale might overwhelm us, or appear mean. Similarly, the lack of any clear location and articulation of a door may make us feel excluded, and an obvious location that lacks symbolic content may be banal. Even skilful use of architectural syntax to articulate the appropriate scale and location of the door will not compensate for a loss of meaning.

The fifth criterion is the idea that new buildings should serve as paradigms for what other buildings, to be erected at some future time on adjacent parcels of land, should be like. For architects, the implication of this principle is obvious: gauge any new architectural or planning idea by assessing what would happen if everyone around you followed your example. It is an architectural version of the biblical injunction not to do to others as you would not have them do to you. The principle was well understood by the architects and developers of Georgian London and Dublin, or 19th-century Boston. It was not so well understood in recent times by those planning authorities in Europe and the United States who have permitted the indiscriminate construction of high-rise buildings in and adjacent to districts that contained only low buildings, or by those leaders of universities who have allowed their campuses to lose their architectural cohesion by permitting construction that lacks any relationship in form or meaning to the existing context. That some of these new buildings were designed by distinguished architects makes the irony sadder still.

This is not to say, of course, that change should not be permitted. On the contrary: change is inevitable and desirable. Nevertheless, it is important for us to distinguish between a genuine need for adjustment, alteration, or even complete reconsideration of a particular paradigm in response to an evolving functional, aesthetic, structural or iconographic need, and mere wilfulness. The latter is usually related to egocentric behaviour by an owner, an architect, a head of state, a municipal government or a commission, behaviour which may substantially damage community well-being or the architectural character of a building, a neighbourhood or a street in the name of profit or the sheer assertion of power.

The process of judging a proposal which is based on changing a paradigm may be likened to the procedures used to review the pros and cons of a new policy or law, with the exception that the aesthetic questions involved add an additional layer of complexity. By exploring the potential benefits, drawbacks and costs to affected and concerned parties, all the different aspects of the proposal may be studied, reviewed and assessed. Judgement should be based on the claim of public purpose. A new paradigm should represent a new synthesis of a building type and expanded knowledge of its purpose, function and character. Paradigms should not be changed unless a compelling reason exists to do so. Thus Lever House

(1952) on Park Avenue in New York is an example of a new but superficial paradigm for office building design. It does not represent a new synthesis of knowledge or new purposes. On the contrary, the architect's preoccupation with self-expression launched the destruction of the street line of Park Avenue, a blight which soon spread to Sixth Avenue, Third Avenue and other important streets throughout the city.

By supplying a common format, which serves to focus discussion on such important questions, these five criteria should be useful in formulating an evaluation of – and, eventually, in framing a response to – the proposal for a new project.

Continuity Versus Contrast: Selecting a Design Strategy
In the context of building in relation to historic architecture or landscape, we are challenged by two opposing design ideals: continuity and contrast. Most critical architectural judgements may be situated among the many shades of grey that lie between these two extreme positions.

Continuity suggests that the new should grow directly from the old, that there should be no break in the development of a historical tradition, of architectural precedent, language or expression. The principle is *not* a prescription for mindless replication of the architecture nearby, but for the new development of relevant ideas and themes. Its goal is to promote integrated growth and development rather than an abrupt break and then a new start which may jar the connection between past and present.

Contrast proposes that because the new, or more often some aspect of it, is different from the old, the relevant design features which express this difference should stand out. This expression should imply a new development which renders some aspect of an existing paradigm obsolete, or in need of modification, so that the design is imbued with new content. The principle differs sharply from modernistic architecture's typical use of contrast, which employs all five criteria – architectural language, syntax, context, symbolic content and role as paradigm – to distinguish new buildings from their surroundings. The purpose, and indeed, the result, of such a sweeping use of contrast is to render the old obsolete or irrelevant in relation to the new. Its use in the history of architecture was infrequent prior to 1950; usually the strategy of contrast is more subtly employed, limited in its application to only a few of these categories.

As design strategies, both continuity and contrast have advantages and drawbacks. It is only by evaluating the particular circumstances of each design project in terms if its architectural language, syntax, context, symbolic content and its role as a paradigm that the choice of which should be expressed by continuity or by contrast can be isolated and discussed. In relating these five criteria to the strategies of contrast and continuity, the preconceptions that surround the project – aesthetic, political and otherwise – can be evaluated fairly, and an informed decision can be reached.

Continuity

Continuity is an architectural response predicated on the further development of, or variation on, some of the principles on which the architecture of a historic district is based. Under the rubric of continuity, a wide range of responses is possible. An extreme example, from 1713, is Sir Christopher Wren's project to restore the north transept of Westminster Abbey. He submitted a design which was 'of a Style with the Rest of the Structure, which I would strictly adhere to throughout the whole Intention'.[6] On the other hand, when Wren completed the 16th-century two-storey base of Tom Tower (1681) at Christ Church, Oxford, he was slightly less respectful, writing, 'I resolved it ought to be Gothick to agree with the Founder's Worke, Yet I have not continued soe busy as he began.'[7] Nicholas Hawksmoor adopted a similar attitude in his design for the completion of the towers of Westminster Abbey's west front (1734).

Like contrast, continuity may be both a conceptual and a formal quality of architecture. This is illustrated by the example of the US Capitol in Washington, DC, where Thomas U Walter's new dome, completed in December 1863, replaced Charles Bulfinch's earlier Pantheon-like structure of 1824. The models for Walter's dome were the great domes of Michelangelo at St Peter's (1590) in Rome and Wren at St Paul's in London, both of which were also inspired by the Pantheon. The US Capitol dome, however, is a secular structure and shelters neither religious nor royal icon. This rotunda is an expression of the democratic ideal that the government is the people and, therefore, belongs to its citizens; as such it is the conceptual centre of the nation, an empty space dedicated to the right of assembly for political or any other purpose. Because in a democracy politicians, ministers and cabinet officers are merely temporary office holders, the chambers that contain the House of Representatives and the Senate are pushed off the Capitol's main axis, respectively to the south and to the north along its cross axis. The President is located in a separate building – the White House – at the other end of Pennsylvania Avenue, which, like the buildings for the various departments of government, is a secondary and tertiary component of the overall plan for the Federal City. These form lesser components within an urban design dominated by the dome of the Capitol.

This is continuity of a high order, as is appropriate for the various institutions of government in a democracy.[8] However, it is also continuity of the ideal of contrast. It was the clear intention of President George Washington that the Capitol be a unique structure, the first domed building in the new republic. The use of both continuity and of contrast in the same building is a more difficult design challenge, but it is one that makes for a richer and more complex formal and iconographic solution.

As an architectural design goal, continuity does not imply that the architecture of a new building should mimic that of the adjacent historic structures, as if the architect of the new structure was a contemporary of those who designed the older ones. On the contrary, this tendency may be characterised as 'traditionalism', a phenomenon that can produce 'kitsch', or such pastiches of architecture as one may find at Disneyland and in historic towns where new buildings by unskilled architects or builders attempt to ape colonial or federal architecture. This process of trying to recreate a lost past by pretending that the immediate past never existed, or is irrelevant, is rooted in sentimentality. Traditionalism is an end, and has nothing to do with tradition, a vital and forward-looking process which enables an architect to isolate the best and most relevant aspects of past and present and to transform them to suit the new demands of the future.

Background Buildings

Continuity is most frequently used to design background buildings. These are buildings housing functions which are similar to those performed in buildings within close proximity, and which therefore lack special importance or public significance. Such buildings seldom warrant special architectural or civic expression on the street, and their architecture is usually understated, employing continuity as an important characteristic. Background architecture is also capable of an extraordinary variety of expression, however. The residential streets and squares of 17th-, 18th- and 19th-century England and France furnish many examples of brilliant background buildings. The government buildings of the Federal Triangle in Washington, DC contrast with commercial and residential areas but use continuity with respect to other governmental structures related to the Mall or Pennsylvania Avenue.

Continuity may not always be an appropriate response. After the Great Fire of 1666, for example, Wren invented a new church form to incorporate changes in Anglican liturgy that had occurred over the previous century – a period in which there was little church construction. Although some of the City churches dating from this era – most of which were designed by Wren – may have reused old foundations, their interior planning and exterior design are adapted to the requirements of the new liturgy, and are quite revolutionary.

Contrast

Contrast is a particularly difficult and challenging design concept to articulate. The tension on which it relies is most potent when the polarity between new and existing buildings is most clearly presented. A diametrical polarity imbues the implementation of contrast with a profound irony: by reacting at 180 degrees to a given context

Sir Christopher Wren, proposal for restoration of north transept facade, Westminster Abbey.

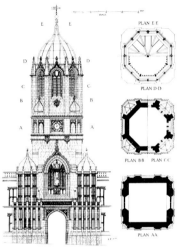

Sir Christopher Wren, Tom Tower, Christ Church, Oxford.

Thomas U Walter, new dome with a cast-iron structure on the U S Capitol.

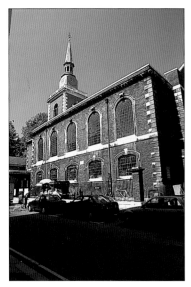

Sir Christopher Wren, St James, Piccadilly, facade facing forecourt.

in order to emphasise the contrast, such buildings depend on exactly those design principles and traditions against which they react. By virtue of this necessarily direct reaction – or opposition – to the tradition, such buildings may also be said to be dependent on that tradition. It is this duality of difference from, and direct dependence upon, the very tradition against which it is reacting that makes contrast as much a conceptual as a physical attribute of architecture.

We tend to think of contrast as the preserve of radical modernistic architects like Le Corbusier. However, one may easily imagine Inigo Jones, for example, writing a set of design notes similar to Le Corbusier's Five Points of modernistic architecture to explain the design of his new Banqueting House (1619), which stood out in stark contrast to the Tudor Palace of Whitehall of which it was a part. It is difficult for us, today, to imagine how this most subtly ordered classical facade designed with three different hues of stone looked in the 1620s, surrounded by a 'jumble' of smaller medieval and Elizabethan buildings.[9] The contrast caused a contemporary critic to state, in 1621, that Jones' addition was 'too faire and nothing suitable to the rest of the house'.[10] The same might have been said about his Queen's House at Greenwich (begun in 1616), or the church, piazzas and housing at Covent Garden (1631). Other examples occur throughout the history of architecture and include such buildings as the New York City Hall (1802-11) by Mangin and McComb, the US Capitol in Washington, DC, as conceived by George Washington and realised by Benjamin Latrobe, and Sir Christopher Wren's Great Model (1674) design for St Paul's Cathedral (1675-1711) in London, as well as his realised building.

The use of contrast should be the exception rather than the rule, and we should not forget that its most potent use may be as an aspect of a building's expressive arsenal. This may be illustrated by the brilliant use of contrast of scale with the surrounding buildings by Gian Lorenzo Bernini to articulate the Piazza of St Peter's, Rome (1667), and by Inigo Jones at St Paul's Covent Garden in London (1630-31). In each case, the contrast of scale is accomplished using classical architectural language and syntax: respectively, by the scale of Bernini's great Doric colonnade and Jones's Tuscan temple front.

We must be aware of the limitations of an exclusive reliance on contrast in urban planning, for it produces the kind of simplistic, additive design which is so characteristic of many new areas of our cities and suburbs. Such a strategy is seldom able to produce the appropriate complexity of response that is usually demanded by urban, rural and even suburban sites.

Foreground Buildings

The use of contrast is most frequently used as an element of the design of foreground buildings. These buildings usually house specific public or religious functions. As such, their architectural and urbanistic expressions are as special or unique structures. Schools, libraries, churches and synagogues, hospitals, statehouses, city halls and firehouses are often free-standing structures and rely on contrast of massing, syntax and, often, architectural language. Foreground buildings also may be placed on sites with limited street frontage, and may then rely on the syntax of the elements of architectural language, such as change of scale, variation of rhythm, or inflection. Alternatively, they may use such features as a tower, an elaborate entrance door, a portico or a dome to achieve this end. Wren's City churches, or McKim, Mead & White's branch libraries in New York, furnish many examples of the ways an architect given limited street frontage may express the importance of foreground buildings.

In assessing the significance of a decision to design a background or foreground building, symbolic content is a particularly important factor to be considered. The mayor of a small town in Vermont located the town hall in a retail building with shops on either side and placed his own office in the display window. By doing so, he undercut the significance of a typical foreground building in order to make citizens feel that the office of the mayor was accessible and its transactions open to public scrutiny. This mayor, like Louis XIV, deliberately chose the place of government and the character of its architecture knowing full well that this would come to represent the nature of government in the public eye. This expression of contrast is one of use rather than architectural design. The storefront branch library in New Haven was established with similar goals in mind. While a more monumental expression of civic importance is often more desirable, the design of a foreground building dictates that architect and client take great care to ensure that both building type and site considerations warrant such particular architectural expression.

The successful use of contrast in a building's design often depends on the subtle expression of its symbolic content. It is not the fact of uniqueness or a special quality that is critical to express, but rather the nature of this quality. Consequently, the authority embodied in a city hall must be qualitatively qualified. The King's authority expressed in Buckingham Palace is different from that of the members of the House of Commons in the Houses of Parliament, as is that of Senators in the Capitol in Washington, and the mayor in the storefront city hall in Vermont. And these are quite radically different from Hitler's authority as depicted in the vast, inhumanly scaled buildings he and Albert Speer planned for the centre of Berlin. Without the quality of precise definition of the nature of the symbolic content, as it is expressed in architectural language and syntax, the use of contrast often reflects mere bombast, as occurs in office buildings with unnecessarily large and grandiose entrances, or implies powerful and often terrifying authority, as in Le Corbusier's plan for the Ville Radieuse. This project was to replace the traditional city – that is, the city as developed from the ancient Greeks' vision of a democratic society, the ancient Roman city of laws, and the Renaissance city of commerce, to our great cities of the 19th and early 20th centuries. If such a vision were to have been plane of reference. This provides the basis for an architect to expand the boundaries of this language or to react against it. In classical architecture it is architectural language and syntax that serve as the constant. Modernistic architecture's canon, however, precludes such constants. It assigns an architectural license to the quality of self-expression alone and uses contrast as a means of differentiating new from old, which means that each new building, or group of buildings, whether on a farm, in a village, or on a city street, is different, both separate and self-referential. The result is the inarticulateness and the sometimes chaotic incoherence which results from the absence of communication.

Analysing and Evaluating New Projects

The opposing forces of contrast and continuity, including the decision of whether the building is a background or foreground design, can be used in conjunction with the five analytical criteria to begin to assess what impact a proposed building, or group of buildings, may have on its context. For the sake of stimulating public discourse, the five criteria may be grouped under the two headings:

CONTINUITY	CONTRAST
architectural language	architectural language
architectural syntax	architectural syntax
context	context
symbolic content	symbolic content
paradigm	paradigm

Clearly, there are many possible combinations of these categories. For example, a building may assert continuity in its language, its role as a paradigm, and its symbolic content, but contrast in its context and syntax. All the possible combinations may be presented by a matrix of these categories. While most of the buildings noted earlier are extreme cases of a focus on either contrast or continuity, most architecture uses combinations of both.

In order to test the validity of this series of critical categories for assessing the merits of building proposals, let us explore two case studies of buildings of widely differing character on historically important sites.

The forecourt of St James Piccadilly (1676-84). Sir Christopher Wren; church restored and tower rebuilt by Sir Albert Richardson (1968).The unassuming forecourt to Wren's beautiful church is defined by two buildings: the Midland Bank (1922) by Sir Edwin Lutyens on one side, and the rectory (1946) by Austin Blomfield on the other. It is separated from the hustle and bustle of Piccadilly by a change of level which is defined by a

fence and gateway through which one passes to enter the forecourt. These are by Sir Reginald Blomfield.

Lutyens orients his bank building to Piccadilly, but also recognises its crucial role defining one side of the space of the forecourt. In order to suggest a relationship between the bank building and the church, he uses similar design features – brick, with stone trim at the windows and doors, and rustication. All three buildings – church, bank and rectory – use red brick, while their immediate neighbours are built of white or cream-coloured stone. This establishes the family of buildings defining the forecourt. Lutyens designed the bank's side elevation with two rows of three high windows. These are the only elements punctuating the brick wall facing the forecourt. There is no articulation at forecourt level, and visitors sense the lack of any functional relationship between bank and forecourt, aware that the latter relates exclusively to the church.

The bank's street facade suggests continuity with the church, for both use arches and rustication, and are built of brick and stone. The bank's design appears overly elaborate next to Wren's austere and monumental side elevation of St James'; Lutyens does this purposely. He followed the example of most of the adjacent commercial buildings on Piccadilly, which vie with each other in their abundance of detail. In this way, he unequivocally relates his design to the life of the street, and away from the forecourt. The tripartite division of the facade and its powerful articulation are inspired by Sanmicheli's great Porta S Zeno (1541-42), Verona.

Thus Lutyens successfully uses contrast of both architectural language – a richly articulated and Italian-inspired version of Wren's simpler and more monumental 17th-century English classicism – and of syntax. The pronounced vertical rhythm and three-dimensional character of the rustication are very different from the simpler and flatter elevation of the church. The expression of similar elements – windows, doors and architraves – is carefully orchestrated to relate Lutyens' building to the street, while balancing its role as the definer of the space of the forecourt. So we see how contrast plays upon differences between various 'dialects' of classical architecture while allowing for the continuity of some elements of syntax.

Lutyens' building served as an appropriate paradigm for the rectory at the opposite end of the forecourt by virtue of its unequivocal commitment to being a background building with respect to defining the space of the forecourt and to providing for continuity of street facade and street life. For St James' Rectory, Austin Blomfield designed a modest building. He wanted it to harmonise with and enhance its setting. Although it uses an austere classical language inspired by Wren's church to articulate its forms, and both church and rectory are constructed of a similar colour and type of stone and brick, the rectory is most certainly not a building Wren might

Sir Edwin Lutyens, Midland Bank Piccadilly, north facade.

Austin Blomfield, rectory of St James Piccadilly, northwest corner.

Sir Reginald Blomfield, wrought-iron fence along Piccadilly.

have designed. For example, the windows over the entrance door are two groups of three-sash units, more characteristic of late-19th- and early-20th-century architecture than of any work by Wren.

Blomfield does not interrupt the site's celebration of the 'Wrenaissance' tradition of English architecture.[11] Continuity is his basic strategy for accomplishing this goal. On the elevation facing Piccadilly, the regular rhythm of the rectory's windows echoes the rhythms of the church's own windows. Similarly, the projecting centre mass of the rectory's forecourt elevation, which focuses attention on the entrance, delicately evokes Wren's use of a different mass of the tower to articulate the church's entrance. The result is continuity of architectural language as well as both continuity and contrast of syntax.

The primary importance of the forecourt is recognised by the placement of the rectory entrance facing the forecourt. The side of the rectory building is set on the street, maintaining the continuity of the building line and the street. Sir Reginald Blomfield's powerful gate piers and elaborate wrought-iron gates facilitate this by strongly defining the plane connecting the rectory with the bank. His generously scaled steps emphasise the lower level of the forecourt and assist in strengthening its distinct identity. By planning the rectory with its major facade as an entrance facing onto the forecourt, and thereby relating it to the church, Austin Blomfield effectively divorces it from the busy commerce on the street. Blomfield's building reverses Lutyens' strategy and thereby enhances the conceptual underpinnings of the composition as well as the rectory's direct response to church and bank.

With disarming simplicity, Blomfield's rectory is able to fulfil its responsibilities as a definer of one side of the church's forecourt while recognising its role as a secondary building. Its subtle facade is a critical element in the change of scale from the larger commercial buildings on Piccadilly to the human scale of the forecourt. Blomfield's side elevation is also a part of the continuous series of elevations which define Piccadilly. Its extreme simplicity and plainness effectively distinguish the rectory from the adjacent commercial buildings.

Le Corbusier, Carpenter Center for the Visual Arts (1960-63)

One of the most eloquent written statements of the power of contrast as a physical and conceptual ideal is Le Corbusier's Five Points of modernistic architecture. This is a codification of the qualities which distinguish his and other International Style buildings from those of the past. Le Corbusier's lucid sketches of his Five Points illustrate the use of *piloti*, continuous bands of windows, roof gardens, and the conventions of free-plan and free-facade. He also sketches the corresponding features of the traditional buildings against which he is reacting. These are buildings dependent on conventional load-

bearing wall structures and on such classical design principles as those exemplified by architects from Iktinos to Soane. (Le Corbusier is careful not to refer to 19th- and 20th-century American classical buildings which use frame construction, as they would undermine the force of his polemic.) Le Corbusier defines his new system in relation to the one it is meant to replace. To that extent, he works in relation to classical ideals and construction systems. However, this relationship is not complementary, but exclusionary. Because Le Corbusier, Gropius and their followers intended to destroy the classical tradition of architecture and urbanism and replace it with International Style architecture and CIAM planning ideals, they should not be considered a part of it.[12]

Le Corbusier uses the Five Points as the basis of his design for Carpenter Center which is set on the Harvard University campus in Cambridge, Massachusetts. The expression of these aesthetic ideals in built form effectively divorces the building from the classical colonial, federal, colonial revival, Victorian, Romanesque revival and American Renaissance buildings which are nearby. The main cubic mass is situated on a diagonal in relation to Quincy Street, on one side, and Prescott Street on the other. An elevated ramp cuts through the centre of the building to connect the sidewalks of both streets. Two curved, sculptural forms on *piloti*, housing studios, bulge out on either side of the cube. The Carpenter Center's monolithic concrete construction no longer celebrates Le Corbusier's technological aesthetic of the 1920s. The concrete is brutal in its purposeful lack of any concession to human tactile sensibility.

Le Corbusier's Five Points emphasise a contrast between a new modernistic architecture which looked forward to creating an industrial aesthetic expressing dynamic freedom rather than static fixity, thinness in place of thickness, lightness where there had been heaviness. Carpenter Center's inversion of the original aesthetic intent of the Five Points evokes a pre-classical past. This was a time when construction was more elemental; the various structural and ornamental parts of a building had not been formed, refined or named. The Doric column with its capital consisting of abacus and echinus and its base of torus and scotia set on a plinth had not yet evolved from a simple post or a pier. The mouldings to articulate transition from one plane to another, such as the architrave, cornice, string course and baseboard, had not been invented. Thus, by contrast, the surrounding architecture appears to be more sophisticated and urbane than the rudimentary forms projected by Le Corbusier's academic building that are reminiscent of a pre-classical past.

The lack of relationship among the disquieting forms and the coarse materials employed at Carpenter Center with those of other buildings on the Harvard campus inhibits or even precludes any effective dialogue between Carpenter Center and it neighbours. On the grounds of an institution dedicated to rational discourse and exchange of ideas, this purposeful lack of dialogue projects a singularly inappropriate and discordant message to faculty and students. This is especially poignant in light of the President of Harvard's brief to Le Corbusier, which stressed the need to invite-in students and faculty from the rest of the university.[13]

This sense of self-imposed isolation is reinforced by the building's problematic intent as a paradigm for the future. Carpenter Center's design makes it a unique structure on the campus. It disrupts the continuity of street line and its main mass is perceived on the diagonal, pulling the viewer's eye away from the street and focusing it on the building. It has no front or rear facade, no obvious designated entrance, or even an entry door. The elevated walkway, which cuts right through the centre of the building, lacks definition as part of the public realm – the street – or the private. Although the two curved, concrete masses on either side of the building eloquently try to mediate between its diagonal cubic core and the adjacent orthogonally sited buildings, they also emphasise its isolation from the fabric of the university.

Carpenter Center is a tour de force of sculptural articulation, but fails as a work of architecture because its symbolic content is ill-considered. By virtue of the power of its use of contrast in architectural language and in context, the architecture asserts that what it contains is a unique programme on the campus, one so special that it is housed in a unique work of architecture that appears to have nothing in common with other university buildings. Yet Carpenter Center houses a visual arts programme, one of dozens of academic departments at the university. The contradiction between immodest assertion and mundane reality cuts the ground out from under the design. Because the building's form lacks the rigour required to successfully satisfy its programmatic requirements, it ends up looking out of place – a quality that is emphasised by the powerful sculptural quality of its articulation.

The ramp is a significant feature of Carpenter Center. It rises above grade and cuts through the centre of the building. Another pathway, a footpath, begins at grade and turning under the ramp, gradually drops below grade – like a drainage channel – to indiscriminately conduct pedestrians through left-over spaces and past parked cars and garbage dumpsters. Despite the importance of the ramp and the pathway in the design, the location of the entrance to Carpenter Center remains an enigma. Le Corbusier's concrete walls serve to shield his building's interior spaces from the world of the university. In this respect, it is the very antithesis of an academic building.

Carpenter Center is a poor paradigm for other architects. It projects a confused message to the next generation of architects. The results may be seen in the two newest buildings on Quincy Street, Gund Hall, the Graduate School of Design (1967-69), by John Andrews, and the Arthur M Sackler Museum (1981) by James Stirling. Both architects are disciples of Le Corbusier and followed the master's example. They use contrast to emphasise the newness and distinction of their own buildings at the expense of relating to the Harvard campus. By doing this, they undercut the power of Le Corbusier's building and further compromise the integrity of Quincy Street and the campus. Carpenter Center needed its immediate environment of traditional buildings to be frozen if it was to maintain the tension of its contrast with the architecture of its neighbours. His successors failed to understand that Le Corbusier wished to be the only modernistic architect in this visual setting. Gund Hall and the Sackler Museum now jostle with Carpenter Center for attention and are themselves equally poor paradigms for future architecture on the Harvard campus and in Cambridge.

Carpenter Center might have been more appropriately planned as a background building, like most buildings at Harvard. The Harvard Yard is a series of spaces defined by buildings, many of which are modest and of indifferent architectural quality. It is the space formed by these background buildings – more than the buildings themselves – which gives the Yard its memorable character. Diagonally opposite Carpenter Center, across Quincy Street, is a composition of three outstanding buildings: Sever Hall (1878) by Henry Hobson Richardson, Robinson Hall (1899) by McKim, Mead & White, and Emerson Hall (1900) by Guy Lowell. All three architects recognised the framework of the Harvard tradition.

Carpenter Center is an offspring of the International Style buildings of the 1920s and 1930s. The buildings of this era were regarded as outposts of a new form of rationally planned city which would eventually replace older cities perceived as obsolete. Grounded in a putative, presumably complete world view, the architecture has at its heart the sharp contrast of the new building with its old environment. As an outpost of the Ville Radieuse, it is a relic of a way of thinking that was outmoded in 1960, and inappropriate for any urban environment, even in the 1920s.

These two case studies of building on an urban street speak to very different general notions of the appropriateness inherent in reliance on tradition. Both teach that this should be violated only in unusual circumstances. In their respective ways, Lutyens and Blomfield strove to ensure that Piccadilly was enhanced by their new buildings, while preserving the integrity of the forecourt to St James'. Carpenter Center's design and symbolic content, on the other hand, make it a building that becomes more difficult to admire with the passage of time. These buildings offer very different sorts of paradigms for future development. One lesson to be derived from study of Carpenter Center is that while it may be acceptable to experiment with intensely personal architectural ideas on sites which are removed from visual contact with neighbours, to do so on a city street or on a university campus

Le Corbusier, Carpenter Center for the Visual Arts, Harvard University, Cambridge, Massachusetts.

Le Corbusier, Carpenter Center, Harvard University, Cambridge, Massachusetts, view across Quincy Street.

William Buckland, Hammond-Harwood House, Annapolis, Maryland, sketch showing facade with all elements of the classical language of architecture removed

may be destructive of urban environments and offensive to many of the citizens and students who must live and work in it. A change in any aspect of an urban architectural paradigm, especially if the building is in a specific setting like a university or a residential square, demands substantial justification.

Conclusion

The ideas presented here are intended to provide a means of structuring discussion and articulating differences in order to make more informed evaluations and studied decisions about proposed new architecture. The hope is that they will help public officials, architects, developers and concerned citizens to conduct their negotiations with greater clarity and to forge compromises more creatively. Only by beginning this difficult task will we be able to

move away from those matters of self-interest, personal taste, and political and aesthetic preferences which debilitate debate about new projects today.

The solutions to the great challenge we face in architecture and physical planning mandate clear thinking and the intelligent use of all our resources. It is only by making distinctions between qualities of architecture, and understanding their relationship to the existing parts of our cities, towns, and rural areas, that we will be able to discuss how best to make considered judgements and achieve a more dynamic and intelligent relationship between new buildings and their settings. This is the architectural challenge that has been bequeathed to us by the architects of the past who designed the cities and towns we so admire today.

Notes

1   I am indebted to Carroll William Westfall, Judith Seligson and William L MacDonald, who read early drafts of this paper and helped me to clarify my ideas, and to Kathryn McCutchen, my assistant, and Sara Blackburn, my editor, for their editorial assistance and endless patience.

2   Blondel's little known work at Metz is discussed in Peter Collins, 'Genius Loci: The Historic Continuity of Cities', *Progressive Architecture*, 44, July 1963, pp100-106.

3   Geoffrey Scott, *The Architecture of Humanism: A Study in the History of Taste*, Boston, 1914, p210. Le Corbusier's definition of 1923 is very similar: 'Architecture is the masterly, correct and magnificent play of masses brought together in light.' Le Corbusier, *Towards A New Architecture*, New York, 1972, p31. Both Scott and Le Corbusier limit the scope of architecture to formal articulation.

4   The pioneering studies of Jane Jacobs, *The Death and Life of Great American Cities*, New York, 1961, and *The Economy of Cities*, New York, 1969, and of Oscar Newman, *Defensible Space: Crime Prevention Through Urban Design*, New York, 1972, focus on the way people live in and use cities and interact with buildings. They offer brilliant insight, and their approach to the study of the city and architecture is of vital importance to practice today.

5   The term 'symbolic content' is used here instead of iconography. Iconography refers to a combination of form, derived from art, and content, derived from literature, theology and other aspects of culture.

6   Viktor Furst, *The Architecture of Sir Christopher Wren*, London, 1956, p60.

7   Margaret Whinney, *Christopher Wren*, New York, 1971, p141.

8   For a more detailed discussion of the plan of Washington, DC, see Allan Greenberg, 'L'Enfant, Washington, and the Plan for the Capital', *The Magazine Antiques*, 140, July, 1991, pp112-23.

9   The facade was refaced by Sir William Chambers and then by Sir John Soane. See Robert Tavernor, *Palladio and Palladianism*, London, 1991, p134. I am indebted to Professor Carroll William Westfall for bringing this to my attention. Also see Edward Jones and Christopher Woodward, *A Guide to the Architecture of London*, London, 1983, p194.

10 John Summerson, Inigo Jones, Harmondsworth, 1966, p57.

11 The term 'Wrenaissance' is used by Christopher Hussey to describe Lutyens' architecture. It acknowledges Lutyens' debt to the work of Sir Christopher Wren. Christopher Hussey, *The Life of Sir Edwin Lutyens*, London, 1950, pp103 and 136.

12 This point has not been recognised by Colin Rowe, whose writings place Le Corbusier within the classical tradition. See *The Mathematics of the Ideal Villa and Other Essays*, Cambridge, Mass., 1982, pp1-27.

13 Eduard F Sekler and William Curtis, *Le Corbusier at Work: The Genesis of the Carpenter Center for the Visual Arts*, Cambridge, Mass., 1978, p50.

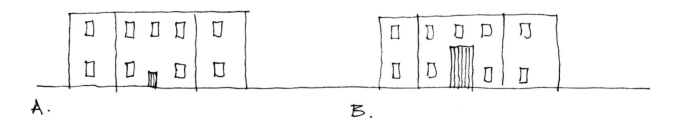

A.

B.

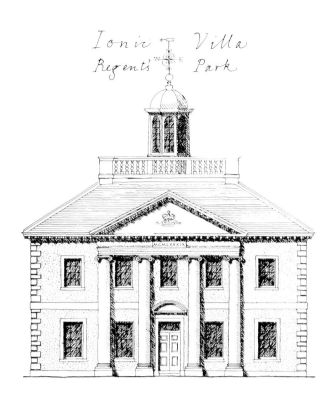

QUINLAN TERRY
THE IONIC VILLA

The Ionic Villa is the first of six Villas commissioned by the Crown Estate Commissioners to be built between the Outer Circle and Regent's Canal on the northwest corner of Regent's Park. Since the work of John Nash is so well exhibited around Regent's Park it was the Crown Estate Commissioners' wish that the new Villas should continue the picturesque tradition.

The Ionic Villa is at the broadest end of the site and therefore has more depth before meeting the slope down to the Regent's Canal. The plan therefore has a narrow front with a greater depth unlike the succeeding Villas. It is based on a design by Andrea Palladio for Signor Gioralamo Ragona at Le Ghissole, published in the Quattro Libri.

The arrangement provides a central staircase in the middle of a 'noughts and crosses' type plan with a three-window-wide Hall leading into the dining room, staircase and drawing room all of which lead onto the loggia. This leaves four spaces in the corners of the plan for the sitting room, study, servery and gents.

This Palladian plan has familiar early Georgian external treatment with sash windows, giant order and slate roof leading up to a balustraded Widows Walk with ornamental lantern, which also lights the central staircase.

The entrance hall, stairs and loggia have stone and slate floors with geometrical patterns together with bold ornamental fireplaces, door surrounds and enriched plaster ceilings. The first-floor accommodation provides a master bedroom suite including bedroom, dressing room and bathroom plus five additional bedrooms and three bathrooms. The service wings provide staff accommodation, double garage and garden shed. The boiler, wine cellar, laundry, etc are in the basement.

The building is constructed in load-bearing brickwork with natural and reconstructed stone dressings and faced in stucco.

ABOVE: NORTHEAST ELEVATION; *BELOW*: NORTHEAST AND SOUTHWEST FACADES

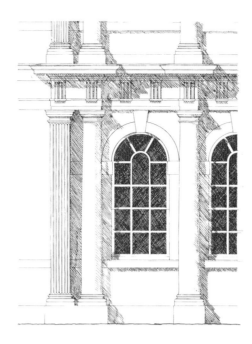

THE VENETO VILLA

The Veneto Villa is the second of the Villas commissioned by the Crown Estate Commissioners. It has a wider frontage with less depth to take account of the different shape of the site. The plan is based on the designs by Andrea Palladio for the Villa Badoer and Villa Zeno. The design has a central staircase and loggia with drawing room and study to the south and dining room and kitchen to the north. The first-floor plan provides six bedrooms and four bathrooms.

This Villa employs a Doric order with a superimposed Ionic Order and parapet on eight columns. The scale is therefore smaller and more refined. This is inspired by the Cornaro Loggia in Padua by GM Falconetto, which was an ideal background for theatrical performances popular in the Veneto. Other Palladian themes popular in the Veneto have been employed; particularly the variation in circular column shaft against fluted pilasters with breaks for projections, all of which are determined by the spacing of triglyphs and metopae in the Doric order and the modillions in the Ionic order.

Internally the detail is English with a strong Veneto influence. This is apparent in the joisted ceilings, Doric pilastered drawing room and the stone and marble floors and fireplaces, which are of a particularly high standard being specially carved by Italian craftsmen to full-size details. The internal treatment continues on the staircase with a lantern supported from domes and pendentives off an Ionic colonnade.

Service wings provide staff accommodation, double garage and garden shed. The basement provides the normal facilities of boiler room, wine cellar, laundry, safe etc.

ABOVE: FACADE DETAIL; *BELOW*: EAST FACADE AND STAIR HALL

THE GOTHICK VILLA

The Gothick Villa, the third of the villas, has a wide frontage with less depth to take account of the narrow depth of the site. The plan is based on the design by Andrea Palladio for the Villa Sarraceno. This was worked up as the initial design for a Tuscan Villa with a castellated pediment and cornice. It was then felt that the design should develop in a more Gothick direction to reflect John Nash's preoccupation with that style. The final design provides a pedimented and castellated front with Gothic orders reminiscent of Gibbs' Temple of Liberty at Stowe employing Batty Langley's Gothic orders. The front door leads into a large hall with marble columns with Corinthian capitals with acanthus leaves springing out of basketwork in the Byzantine manner, and a marble floor inspired by a mosque in Cairo. This in turn leads through to an irregular octagonal loggia with Gothic windows and fireplace and vaulted ceiling influenced by the Gothick work of Soane. The inspiration for much of the detailed work are Nash's Longner Hall and Combermere Abbey, Shropshire which was one of the foremost Gothick buildings in the Strawberry Hill style. The balustrade to the terrace is influenced by Palazzo Contarini-Fasan in Venice and indeed the Venetian precedent of a classical plan with Gothic treatment has been the main theme of the whole design. The ceiling, the dome and pendentives to the staircase hall have obvious counterparts in the fullsome, almost Baroque, details of Spanish Gothic Cathedrals.

The accommodation on the ground floor is similar to the accommodation for the Ionic and Veneto Villas but with a larger Loggia overlooking the Canal.

ABOVE: DETAIL OF CAPITAL; *BELOW*: FRONT FACADE

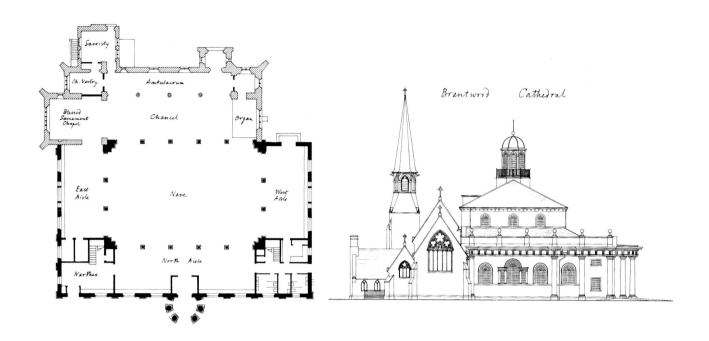

ABOVE L TO R: PLAN, ELEVATION; *BELOW:* INTERIOR VIEW

THE NEW BRENTWOOD CATHEDRAL

The first building that was used as a Catholic Church on this site was an early-19th-century brick building now occupied by the Social Centre. Later in the 19th century a stone Gothic Revival building was erected. When the Church became a Cathedral it was extended by a large modern building in the 1970s built in reinforced concrete.

I was originally approached to improve the interior within the concrete structure. But it was decided that it would be in the interest of the Church to demolish the modern extension and erect a higher building.

The new Cathedral is built alongside the Gothic Revival Church to form an elongated Maltese Cross plan, the old Nave becoming the Chancel with transepts on all four sides. In the Nave the spacing of the columns is dictated by the existing column shafts which remain on the south side but were removed in the modern extension, they have now been replaced. The arches rest on simple Tuscan columns forming an arcade supporting the whole of the central space. At the corners of this arcade are coupled giant Doric pilasters with entablature, complete with triglyphs and metopes which run round the whole of the central space: this is also the main architectural element of the exterior.

Externally, the same giant Doric order is expressed by pilasters on the north and west elevations. The centre bay of the main entrance on the north elevation forms a portico inspired by the south portico of St Paul's Cathedral and St Mary-le-Strand.

Architecturally, the inspiration is early Italian Renaissance crossed with the English Baroque of Christopher Wren. The Doric order is Bramantesque Palladian; the arcade is obviously influenced by Brunelleschi and the cupola is inspired by Bernini's Church in Ariccia. However, the windows have characteristically English lead cames fixed to bronze saddle bars with small panes; the clerestorey is Smeed Dean brickwork, the roof is Welsh slate. The juxtaposition of classic and Gothic elements in the west elevation, and the view of Gothic arches seen through a classical arcade are inevitable in any building which has a long history.

All five orders have been employed in the design; Tuscan for the arcade, Doric for the main giant order, Ionic for the east and west Serlian windows, Composite and Corinthian for the organ and cathedra. The organ case employs a major and minor Corinthian order in timber complete with modillions, coffers and entablature, all gilded.

ABOVE: CROSS SECTION; *BELOW*: NORTH ELEVATION

DIMITRIS A FATOUROS
CLASSICAL REALITY AND CONTEMPORARY CLASSICIST EXPRESSION

The persistent reappearance of the architecture of Classicism in the contemporary scene, with its many facets and pretexts calls for a careful discussion of classical architecture in its setting, that is, of the ancient Greek world.[1] To undertake a comparison of contemporary classicist expression with the Greek classical architecture, at least four points should be carefully and systematically considered: actual suggestions; the Neo-Classicism of the last century; the architecture of the Roman era, and lastly classical architecture in its setting, that is, the Greek classical architecture from the fourth century BC onwards, what we may call *classical reality*. Our discussion here will focus on Greek classical architecture, on classical reality, although only certain of its characteristics will be emphasised – those particularly related to space.

What is the relation between contemporary forms of classicist architecture and classical reality? It would suffice to indicate here that reference to classical architecture today is made through three motifs or characteristics: special stylistic elements, such as the pediment, the column and their style, Ionic, Doric, Renaissance etc, what I call *micro-geometry*; some typological solutions such as the portico and the atrium; and the organisation of space in general, characterised mainly by axial, symmetrical solutions in closed, centralised order.

Typological solutions, such as the portico and atrium are elaborate spatial issues, historically charged. If they are to be used as diachronic qualities they should be reduced to simpler space issues and be discharged from their historical transformation. They should be reduced to pre-typological issues which I call *space morphomes*[2] and they may constitute diachronic features. The integration of the stylistic elements with the spatial arrangement or spatial organisation seems to contribute decidedly to the identity of each era. This is why spatial organisation should be explored and its characteristics identified.

Spatial organisation signals the above two distinctive features, shaping the main criterion of identity and is perhaps the element that carries diachronic quality. A question is therefore raised: are the characteristics of spatial organisation in classical architecture simply or mainly axial solutions and symmetrical arrangements, as contemporary but also older references to them suggest? This is the issue that the present paper will undertake to explore. I will pursue it by analysing three architectural works, three cases in classical Athens: two examples of the fourth century BC, the large complex of the Acropolis

and the small complex of Pompeion, and another of the first century BC, Asklepieion.[3]

The Acropolis

The Parthenon is the largest building, the most significant, symbolic presence on the Acropolis which is a complex of closed, semi-open and open spaces. Nevertheless the Parthenon, whilst being the biggest building and relatively the most detached compared to the other architectural items, is definitely part of a set of buildings and other architectural elements and is part of the architectural whole of the Acropolis. What is called the Parthenon harmoniously integrates with the elements of space that are directly related to it. It is thus a part of them. Not only is it approached in relation to the other elements of the wider area, but the work itself is composed with the elements of its immediate space.[4] The same also applies for the other buildings of the Acropolis, such as the sanctuary of Diana (Artemis) and the Erechtheion.

The design of a building today in the style of the Parthenon without its incorporation, its interrelation and coexistence with the immediate surrounding space, both built and open-air, as this is reflected in the case of the Acropolis, does not constitute, and is not, a proposal of Greek classical architecture. Within the framework of classical reality, every building exists only up to a certain extent autonomously. The building exists within its immediate environment, it is part of a built micro-tissue, an organised space that belongs to it.[5]

Each and every one of the buildings on the Acropolis, ie the Parthenon, Erechtheion etc, is a system or a cohesive whole of buildings, penthouses, courtyards with high walls, sacred presents, statues and elevated and 'sunken' levels.[6] The whole of the Acropolis is a broader unit with the same characteristics, a sum of correlations, attitudes, routes, passages. These constitute inviolate elements of spatial organisation. They are distinctly evident even in the Parthenon, which is the main, symbolic and major construction.

In the ground plan of the whole of the Acropolis the following observations can be made: Seven areas are closed yards and two semi-closed. Eight buildings or small building complexes, temples etc, are situated within these yards directly related to the courtyard walls which surround and define them. Diana's temple, for example, is built like a monastery. The three bigger yards one, two and three are approximately the same size and they divide and organise the whole space of the Acropolis into transitional intermediate areas.

The smaller yards four, five, six, seven and eight have the same organisational relationship to the building or the complexes co-ordinated with them. Yard six, where the Erechtheion is situated, is strongly co-ordinated, in some way subdivides the big yard being one of its subsets. These yards are transitional areas, elements of both the partial work-building and the whole space of the Acropolis. They are integral elements for any movement related to the building, for its very perception, understanding and livelihood. Access to the buildings is not axial, entrances to the closed yards are not in symmetrical positions.

Focusing on the Parthenon first, the main passage to the Parthenon is a typical example of the spatial organisation that I am trying to describe. Since it concerns the movement towards the important temple-symbol, it bears a very crucial significance. One could consider that it denotes the way any classical building *should* be defined, that is, where it starts and where it stops, specifying its borders, its boundaries. The relationship of the work to the whole territory of the Acropolis becomes obvious to the person that passes the entrance when he or she goes through the 'transparent' area of the Propylaea.

Leaving the Propylaea behind, one can see the walls of the courtyards and on the right, through them, part of the Parthenon, eccentrically both in relation to the point of departure and to the course of direction.

Orientation to the main building, the Parthenon, is firstly set by the tall walls of the courtyard of Diana's (Artemis') temple and then by a narrow passage between the courtyard walls of Chalkothiki, the south of courtyard one and the elevated level of the Parthenon.

The exit from Propylaea towards the ground area of the Acropolis and thus towards the Parthenon leads to a fairly large open-air space, the ground area of a square or a 'piazza', the length of which approximately equals that of the Parthenon. The course of movement runs through this piazza, follows the narrow path between the courtyard walls mentioned before and is set by the big wall of the grounds of yard one.

The edifice of the Parthenon itself is defined by these walls and is integrated with Chalkothiki and its grounds and the elevated level with the steps on top of which the Parthenon is located. When movement through the narrow path ends, the Parthenon appears, not only axially but from the left end of the building, from the steps, on the right of the visitor who has come through Propylaea. The pattern of the arrangement is not axial.

Diana's temple demonstrates very definite characteristics of spatial organisation. The main theme-building, the portico, is part of the whole that is composed together with the closed yard and an outbuilding. Entrance to the building is eccentric in relation to both the portico and the yard grounds. In fact the front of the yard on the square follows the direction of the main course towards the Parthenon.

For the Erechtheion as well as the small Pandrosio temple one does not need to persist in the analysis and understanding of the characteristics of space. They constitute a typical example with split levels, yards, various porticos, eccentric entrances and movements as well as asymmetrical arrangements.

The descriptions above illustrate the fact that both the whole spatial organisation of the Acropolis and each one of the items, ie the *co-ordinated entities*, gives emphasis and priority to intermediate space boundaries[7] and asymmetrical arrangements. It is for this reason that passages, to a greater or lesser extent, expose and open up the main theme-building as well as the other buildings, if any, and as well as the interior, 'hidden', open-air spaces of a yard.

Pompeion

A small entity of the fourth century BC, the main and predominant theme of the Pompeion is the peristyle. Entrance is eccentric through the southeast narrow side and the small closed rooms, sacred chambers for therapy etc, are extensions asymmetrically organised against both sides of the external boundary wall. Apart from the entrance gate, there are three more doors all built in asymmetrical positions.

Asklepieion

Built in the first century BC, the Asklepieion is also a small complex. It is a system, an entity of closed, integrated spaces, porticos, yards and passages asymmetrically organised.

The propylon, the entrance to Asklepieion, sets the main movement on the right and perpendicular to the entrance. Movement passes through a door opening and reaches the narrowest part of the yard *before* this 'movement', that is, the person moving notices the big yard. The yard is set by two buildings with pillars, two porticos – a main and a secondary one – and by walls. Entrance to the yard seems to pass off not only through the main propylon but also through a door in the south side of the wall-limit of the courtyard and finally through a small opening in the east. All these passages are eccentric.

The main portico presents asymmetrical organisation and asymmetrical 'extensions' regarding both their arrangement and their geometry; one, the sacred fountain, being round and the other, the altar, being square. The latter has also split levels, an interior elevated level, ie an intermediate space limit.

Concerning the architecture of this classical building the following characteristics could also be noted: The porticos are not identical. The main portico has double depth, with a double row of round pillars, while the second has shallow depth and square pillars. These 'double' porticos and the differences in neighbouring porticos characterises other eras too, for instance, Byzantine architecture.

The floors have split levels and there are four different categories of entrance passages. Asklepieion is an aesthetic whole of space-space and visual organisation.

Conclusions and Implications

Classical reality: An architecture with intermediate boundaries and space distribution involving exploration, concealment and revelation.

The example of the Acropolis alone describes classical reality. The two other examples simply affirm it and demonstrate the same characteristics on a smaller scale:

Space distribution in hidden and open spaces, utilisation of eccentric passages, crooked line paths all indicating priority of psychological over physical time, exploration, partial or complete space revelation[8] behind built items and formations, such as levels-walls, masses, split levels. The application of what I call intermediate space boundaries is indeed evident.

Classical reality then has been designed by neither European historical Neo-Classicism nor contemporary architecture of any Neo-Classicism, the contemporary 'classical' formulation.

Classical reality corresponds more, if it does not completely identify with the syntactical elements, the spatial organisation of Mediterranean villages of the Middle Ages and elsewhere. The way classical reality is defined with a high degree of complexity involving processes of exploration and revelation cannot become a model, cannot be applied to express authoritarian regimes. Only its misunderstanding and reduction to over-simplified and impoverished typological and stylistic qualities permitted its application by totalitarian regimes.

The building coexists with and is restructured by the immediate elements.

A work of architecture, the building itself, even if it is the main building, is always part, an element, of the work entity. If so, the spatial organisation of a building may, for instance, be symmetrical, but by way of its correlation, that is, its coexistence with the other parts or elements of the work, it is transformed and a new 'situation' originates. And it is only within this context that the building exists. The constituent elements with which the work-entity is organised, such as the walls of the courtyard, the altars and the porticos restructure or capsize the arrangement of the main building as well as the other buildings, if there are any, of the architectural work. This seems to be the rule. One may suppose that this rule reflects the intention of the architectural logic governing classical reality.[9]

We may therefore establish that the architectural work, be it of a large or small scale, is not the sheath, the 'biased' and limited shell of a building but a smaller or larger entity – a whole.

This work has an asymmetrical and generally complex internal structure with clearly contrasting principles: at different 'times' of its existence, different perceptual arrangements prevail. Distinctions, explanations and classifications for these categories would be undoubtedly useful but I am not pursuing these issues here.

These findings expose the main characteristics of the typological structure of classical architecture. Its typological identity permeates the whole work and not only part of it, for instance, the larger or most important part, since worship rituals take place indiscriminately everywhere in the edifice. There prevails a unity defined by the elements of the work: the courtyard, the building(s), the semi-covered or semi-open spaces, the open spaces and the altars and other elements of worship of smaller scale. This work unity has a non-axial access to and from the exterior area. We are dealing then with quite a different typology from the uniform, usually centralised and symmetrical building, suggested by the re-establishment of 'Classicism'.

Looking at a deeper level of synthesis and organisation, we may argue that classical architecture uses morphomes of space independent of centralised and symmetrical order, in direct proportion to a complicated, intricate and ambiguous organisation. It grants them poetic potential.

The ornament is not an ornament, it is a microcosm.

The employment of special geometrical characteristics, of micro-geometry as I call the stylistic attributes, the so-called ornaments, does not qualify to give a name to architecture. Indeed, micro-geometry in the eyes of our contemporaries often disregards, perhaps unintentionally, the vital symbolic function of spatial organisation and the reading of space.

Ornaments constitute a microcosm, are characteristic of the small scale and were decisive in the way the architectural work was experienced at its time. They are not ornaments. This microcosm is part of the myth, of the cosmos of the times. It is the surrounding natural and animal world and their symbolic significance. The helix of the plant, the sphinx etc, the symbolic transformations of the structure, such as the mouldings, triglyph etc, contribute along with others to its identity. They stress characteristic traits, joints, interrelations, compose the 'reflections' of substance in the environment, that is, the transformations of the material and the structure through their relation with the relatively recent history and the relations of man with the myths of the pagan world. They are indispensable in defining the typical morphological identity of the work in its period and its dialogue with the society of its time, part of a ceremonial procedure.

The ornament and generally the stylistic characteristics do not constitute the language of classical architecture as regularly as it is presented. The classical language of architecture is the synthesis of space, the organisation of space that I am trying to present.

The so-called stylistic characteristics are always composed, interwoven with the organisation of space-space, since the architectural work is an experienced whole, way and condition of life. It composes a place including the ceremony and the myth as they are shaped by the societies of the period and their culture. It represents in this respect as well a completely different instance and entity from historical Classicism of the 18th and 19th century and from contemporary Classicist or Neo-Classicist expression. Following this way of thinking, the spatial organisation is the diachronic characteristic and the ornament the expression of the cultural, ceremonial identity of the period.

Finally, how would a classical work or architecture, eg the Erechtheion, be different if each one of its elements and traits, such as distribution, intermediate areas, boundaries etc were the same, and only the style, the ornament, varied? If for instance the style were a simple, rectangular system? I will not bring up this issue at present. This simple allusion will do.

A part of the material of this paper first appeared in the form of a lecture during the Conference on Relativism at the School of Architecture of the Architectural Association of London in May 1987 and at the School of Architecture of Cincinnati University in April 1989.

Notes

1 M Greenhalgh, *What is Classicism?*, Academy Editions, London, 1990.

2 DA Fatouros, 'Space Morphomes', *Design and Art in Greece* 22, 1991, and DA Fatouros, *Elements from an Architectural Syntax* (in press).

3 J Travlos, *Pictorial Dictionary of Ancient Athens*, Thames and Hudson, London, 1971.

4 K Doxiadis' study, his doctoral dissertation in Berlin in 1937 explores with geometrical rulings some of the relations among the buildings. KA Doxiadis, *Architectural Space in Ancient Greece*, MIT Press, Cambridge, Mass, 1972. It first appeared in German, *Raumordnung in Griechischen Städtebau*, Vowinkel, Heidelberg, 1937. See also the presentation by D Pikionis, 'E Theoria tou Architectonos KA Doxiadi gia ti Diamorphosi tou Chorou is tin Archaea Architectoniki' (The Theory of the Architect KA Doxiadis about the Formulation of Space in Ancient Architecture), *The Third Eye*, 7-12, 1937.

5 Indeed, it is for this reason that the whole space territory is considered sacred and goes by the common name of *temenos*. Temenos means 'a piece of land cut off with a wall and assigned for a god'. Temenos may be literally translated as a section of land transformed into a sacred place. Let me add here that the root word of temenos is the verb *temno*, which means to cut. For an architectural approach of temenos, see GP Lavas, *Altgriechisches Temenos: Baukörper and Raumbildung*, Birkhauser, Basel, 1974.

6 The significance of courtyard walls, sacred presents and elevated levels for the composition of space in Greek classical architecture was discussed in a systematic manner by RD Martiensen, *The Idea of Space in Greek Architecture*, Johannesburg, 1941; Witwatersrand University Press, 1958.

7 DA Fatouros, *E Organosi tou Chorou ke e Geometriki Organosi* (The Organisation of Space and Geometrical Organisation), Thessaloniki, 1979, and DA Fatouros, *Elements from an Architectural Syntax*, ibid.

8 We may relate these characteristics to what we call exploratory behaviour. This is a well-known constituent of the aesthetic object . . . DE Berlyne, *Conflict, Arousal and Curiosity*, McGraw-Hill, New York, 1960, and DE Berlyne, 'Aesthetic Behaviour and Explanatory Behaviour,' *Acte 5th International Conference on Aesthetics*, Amsterdam, 1964.

9 A Tzonis and L Lefaivre, *Classical Architecture: The Poetics of Order*, MIT Press, Cambridge, Mass, 1986. Even on small scale and in partial characteristics, the pillar, colonnade, mouldings, Tzonis and Lefaivre detect the poetics of an order that is indirect and elaborate.

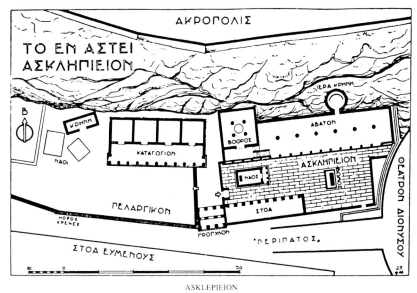

ASKLEPIEION

TOWER DETAIL

DEMETRI PORPHYRIOS ASSOCIATES
BELVEDERE FARM, ASCOT

This commission, currently under construction, comprises a complex of agricultural, residential, office and stable buildings which form a village within the Belvedere Estate near Ascot. The 16 buildings of the village are organised around courts and squares that form an urban environment within the surrounding farmland in a manner similar to a traditional English hamlet. The overall layout and the massing for the buildings have been arranged through careful perspectival planning so that sequences of space and vistas are formed. The

character of the buildings, wedded to the expressiveness of construction, reminds us that traditional buildings are not the monopoly of one particular age but may arise at any time and endure with time. Traditional materials have been used throughout: second-hand mixed London and Surrey stocks for the brickwork; second-hand York stone for the paved areas; Bath stone for the window surroundings of the Hall and for fireplace surroundings; clay tiles, slates and lead sheeting for the roofs; and English oak for all exposed timber work and joinery.

OPPOSITE: DOVECOTE TOWER AND STABLES; *ABOVE*: MAIN BARN; *BELOW*: WEST ELEVATION

ABOVE: ENTRANCE TO NEW QUADRANGLE; *BELOW*: OVERALL VIEW OF THE COURT

MAGDALEN COLLEGE, OXFORD
NEW LONGWALL QUADRANGLE

This is the winning entry in a limited architectural competition. Our proposal for a new quadrangle at Magdalen College, Oxford, comprises residential accommodation for students and fellows, a lecture theatre and an underground car park. The architecture establishes a dialogue between the Magdalen vernacular of the residential buildings and the classico-vernacular of the theatre. The new quadrangle comprises individual buildings which come together in a picturesque medievalising manner while adopting the open quad form of Magdalen College. Our design demonstrates how traditional architecture can create a design of high quality, sympathetic to the context of the historic centre of Oxford.

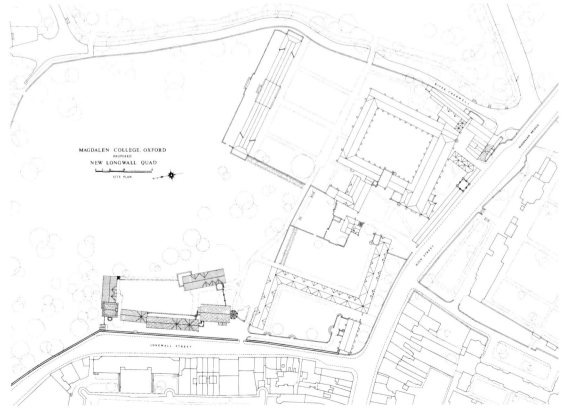

ABOVE: AERIAL PERSPECTIVE; *BELOW:* SITE PLAN

ABOVE: ENTRANCE FACADE; *BELOW*: GARDEN TERRACE

JOHN SIMPSON & PARTNERS
ASHFOLD HOUSE

Ashfold House in Ashfold Park is designed as a small country house, compact and practical for everyday use but nevertheless with the grace and proportion of an 18th-century mansion.

The building is square in plan, each facade responding to its orientation and internal arrangement. A semi-circular bay incorporates a breakfast room on the east, a square conservatory faces west and a long drawing room runs the full length of the south side of the house overlooking the terrace and the park. The approach from the north reveals a facade the design of

which is a paraphrase of a triumphal arch.

The obvious precedent for the house is Sir John Soane's Pitzhanger Manor, Ealing. It has, however, a much more Palladian symmetrical plan arranged around a two-storey rooflit domed central hall with an octagonal library at the upper level.

All the interior furnishings and some of the furniture have been designed with particular attention to detail, including the light switches and sockets which have been specially designed.

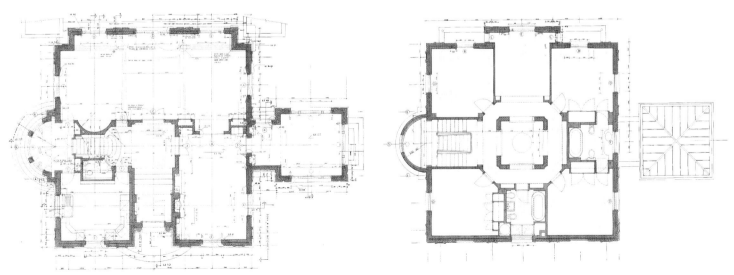

ABOVE: ENTRANCE HALL; *BELOW*: GROUND AND FIRST-FLOOR PLANS

ABOVE: INTERIOR OF DOME; *BELOW*: SITTING ROOM

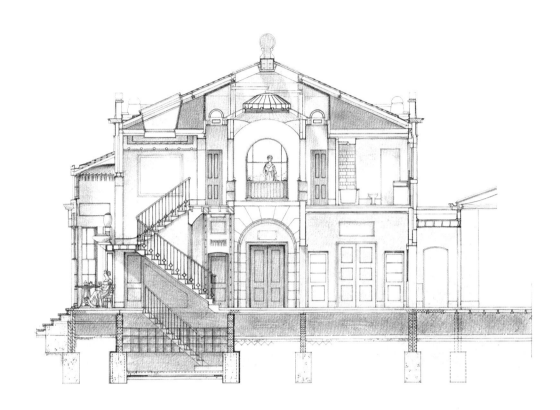

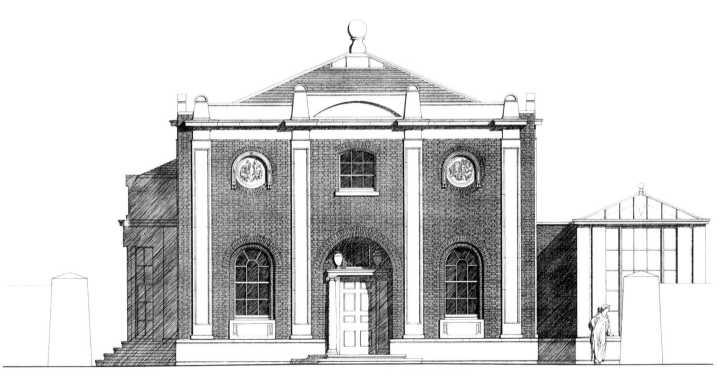

ABOVE: CROSS SECTION; *BELOW*: ENTRANCE ELEVATION

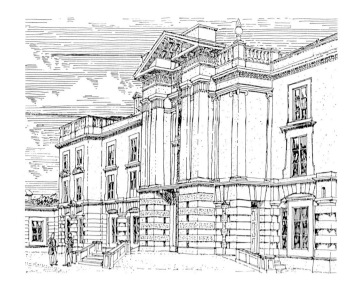

ROBERT ADAM

GOLF CLUB, WEST WRATTING, CAMBRIDGE

A new clubhouse with accommodation for a golf club is to be created on farmland near Cambridge. The design and concept is that of a country house, the club will be strictly limited membership. The specific golfing facilities are housed in one pavilion wing with the opposite wing containing the restaurant, bar and kitchens. The reception rooms are on the ground floor,

two floors of individual suites above and staff accommodation in the attic. There is car parking for 100 cars in the basement.

The park, in which the building is set, will contain a 27-hole golf course set in woodland, grassland and lakes. The design will include a lakeside pavilion, bridges and, in the interior, specially designed furniture.

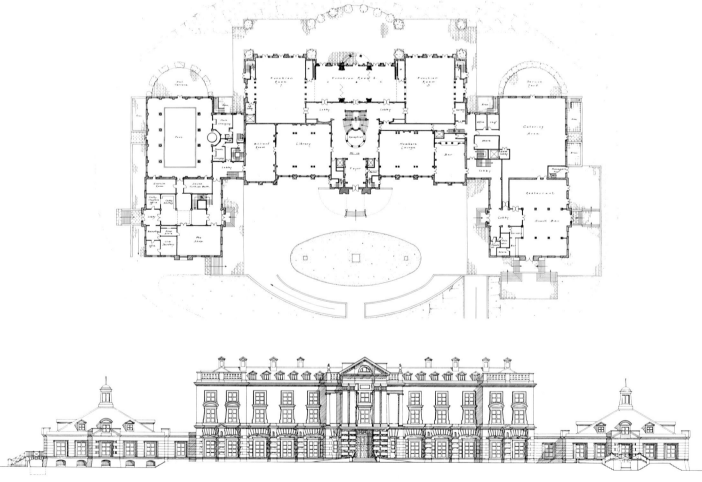

ABOVE: PERSPECTIVE VIEW OF ENTRANCE FACADE; *CENTRE*: GROUND-FLOOR PLAN; *BELOW*: ENTRANCE ELEVATION

NEW HOUSE ON AN ESTATE IN HAMPSHIRE

The house, for a Country Estate in a village in Hampshire, is designed to conform to strict local authority planning constraints largely dictated by the plan area of an existing bungalow and the condition that it must be a single-storey dwelling with all first-floor accommodation in the roof.

The construction is of clay soft brick with terracotta details and a hand-made tile roof with terracotta finials. The doorcase and other details are in hardwood with special carved brackets and other features around the front door.

The entrance front is landlocked having no outlook, while the opposite elevation utilises the fact that it faces out onto open farmland.

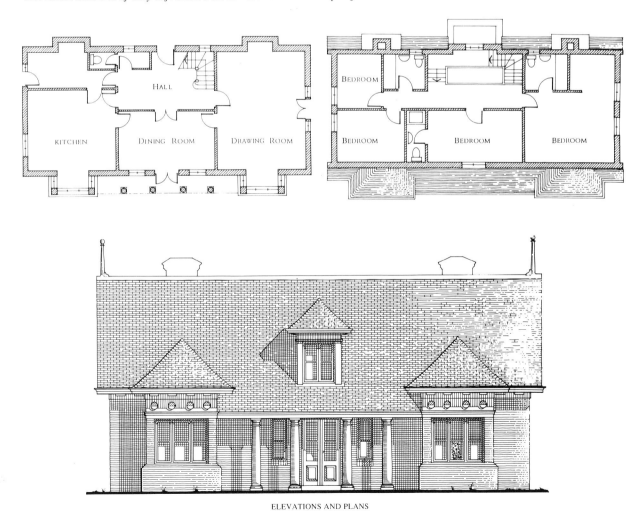

ELEVATIONS AND PLANS

ABOVE: VIEW OF BUILDING IN CONTEXT; *BELOW*: WINTER GARDEN

HAMMOND, BEEBY & BABKA
HAROLD WASHINGTON LIBRARY CENTER

The Harold Washington Library Center will serve as the central library for the City of Chicago. The ten-storey, 760,000-square-foot building is on a site bounded by State Street, Congress Parkway, Van Buren Street and Plymouth Court.

The design intends to inform the user of its role as a public building. The general aspect, use of materials and imagery are combined to remind the user of other public buildings in Chicago that are at once familiar and understandable. The use of ornamentation fulfils its traditional role of breaking down the scale of the building to human dimensions while establishing the degree of monumentality appropriate for a civic structure.

The interior organisation is a result of the Library's demand for a highly flexible typical floor plan that also encourages the visitor's sense of spatial definition. The solution begins with the obvious fact that a building is fixed at its perimeter as well as its top and base, and that the central block of the building offers the greatest opportunity for flexibility.

The building, therefore, has been designed with a base and top largely composed of special public spaces, with the principal library spaces in the central block of the building. To further the concept, fixed elements have been pulled to the perimeter of the building to provide a large flexible floor plan.

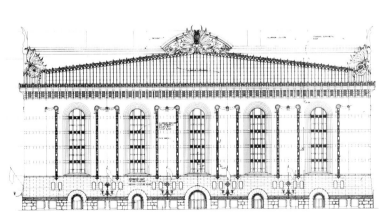

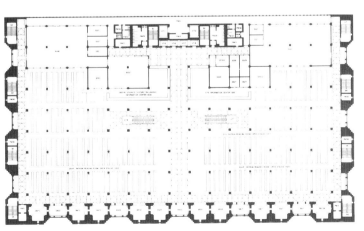

ABOVE: FACADE DETAIL; BELOW: ELEVATION AND PLAN

ALLAN GREENBERG

J WILSON NEWMAN PAVILION, UNIVERSITY OF VIRGINIA

This classically designed addition to the Miller Center acknowledges the restrained classicism which characterises the Faulkner House and the architectural heritage of the region. In particular, Bremo in Fluvanna County, Virginia, and Jefferson's 'Academical Village' at the University have provided inspiration and architectural precedent for the design. The Forum addition, designed as a three-bay pavilion with a Tuscan portico, is linked to the Faulkner House by a two-storey hyphen. The upper storey of the hyphen, a three-bay glazed colonnade, rests on a brick base.

The two-storey addition includes a large assembly room (the Forum), a reception room, two seminar rooms, offices, a catering kitchen, rest-rooms, and two terraces for outdoor events and social gatherings. An elevator in the Pavilion provides the first two floors of the existing building with access for the handicapped. The Forum, a half-panelled assembly room, was inspired by the panelled interiors of the reconstructed Capitol in Williamsburg, and of colonial and early Federal courthouses and churches throughout Virginia.

ABOVE: FRONT FACADE; *BELOW*: FRONT ELEVATION

PERSPECTIVE

THE NEWS BUILDING, ATHENS, GEORGIA

Athens, Georgia is renowned for its Greek Revival architecture and stately porticos. The brief was to design a building to enhance the city. In this way the News Building establishes an appropriate paradigm for the development of downtown Athens.

The press in the United States is often acknowledged as the fourth branch of government. Its architecture should reflect its role as a critical forum to review actions of executive, legislative and judicial branches of government and to inform citizens of these actions. Newspaper buildings are therefore often important structures in a city. The News Building in Athens serves two newspapers, the Athens Banner-Herald *and the* Athens Daily News, *both owned by Athens Newspapers Inc.*

The entrance facade of the News Building has a two-storey doric portico as its central feature. The proportions of the columns and the antae are inspired by the fine doric order at the beautiful Medical College in nearby Augusta. The portico is stone; the walls, brick and the windows, industrial sections.

The metal curtain wall behind the columns is recessed to create an exterior vestibule; this leads to the main public space which provides visitors with access to all of their destinations in the building. The orders are doric and ionic with polychrome treatment which recalls that used on temples of ancient Athens.

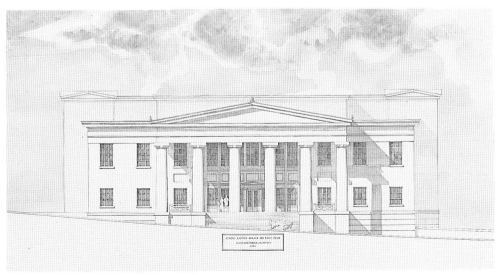

ABOVE: ENTRANCE FACADE; *BELOW*: VIEW OF LOBBY

THE IONIC ORDER, THE NEWS BUILDING, DETAIL